Wonderful Words of Life

Favorite Hymns, Stories and Meditations

by

George W. Wiseman

First Fruits Press
Wilmore, Kentucky
c2012

ISBN: 9781621710325

Wonderful Words of Life: Meditations Based on Traditional Hymns and Gospel Songs, George W. Wiseman
First Fruits Press, © 2012
Previously published by the Author, c1985.

Digital version at http://place.asburyseminary.edu/firstfruitsbooks/6/

For all other uses, contact:

First Fruits Press
B.L. Fisher Library
Asbury Theological Seminary
204 N. Lexington Ave.
Wilmore, KY 40390
http://place.asburyseminary.edu/firstfruits

Wiseman, George W.
Wonderful words of life : meditations based on traditional hymns and gospel songs / George W. Wiseman.
Wilmore, Ky. : First Fruits Press, c2012.
ix, 139 p. ; 21 cm..
Reprint. Previously published: Lake City, Fla. : G.W. Wiseman, c1985.
ISBN: 9781621710325 (pbk.)
1. Methodist Church -- Meditations. 2. Hymns, English – History and criticism. I. Title.
BV4805 .W57 2012

Cover design by David Roux

asburyseminary.edu
800.2ASBURY
204 North Lexington Avenue
Wilmore, Kentucky 40390

Wonderful Words of Life

Favorite Hymns, Stories and Meditations

George W. Wiseman

Wonderful Words of Life

Wonderful Words of Life

Meditations based on traditional hymns
and gospel songs

George W. Wiseman

318 Brady Circle
Lake City, Florida 32055

Printed by
Storter Printing Company, Inc.
Gainesville, Florida

TO OUR ONLY GRANDDAUGHTER
AMY KATHERINE CHAPMAN

CONTENTS

1. ALL HAIL THE POWER OF JESUS' NAME

"His eyes were as a flame of fire, and on his head were many crowns." (Rev. 19:2)

It is always a sad moment when friendships cool. John Wesley had many such experiences which were expected of a strong leader, especially when involved in a new religious movement. One of Wesley's very dear friends was the Rev. Vincent Perronet, Vicar of Shoreham. Upon that friend's death, the Methodist leader said, "O, that I may follow him in holiness; and that my last end may be like his!"

Perronet had two sons, one of whom was Edward Perronet, (1726-1792) who had planned to enter the Anglican ministry. Instead, he and his brother became itinerant preachers of the early Methodist movement. Edward was only 23 when he accompanied Wesley on a preaching tour and they faced angry mobs together, suffered painful bruises and were ridiculed and scorned. This only drew them closer together. However, some years later that friendship cooled when Perronet continued to condemn the Anglican Church. The breach widened when Wesley made it a rule that only the Established Church ministers could administer the sacraments. John Wesley never left the Established Church, even though its doors were closed against him. Soon a split resulted and that intimate friendship ended. Shortly after, Perronet left the Wesleys and became pastor of a small church of Dissenters in Canterbury. He was, however, a sincere, pious individual and before his death wrote one of the great hymns of the church. Dr. John Rippon added two stanzas to the hymn.

All hail the Power of Jesus' name!
Let angels prostrate fall,
Bring forth the royal diadem,
And crown Him Lord of all.

* * * * * * *

At the close of a most trying day, as I was about to leave the hospital, a young man approached and inquired about a critically ill loved one. I told him that at the moment there was nothing new or more encouraging. After further words of comfort he put his hand on my shoulder and said, "Preacher, don't forget that Chap you preach about every Sunday." These were electrifying words, not that I had forgotten, but because this young man in his own way, recognized the power that rested in Jesus. Faith in "that chap" is not only needed in life's crisis hours, but in every experience of life. When discouragement, sickness, or sorrow momentarily overwhelms us, may we remember the power of Jesus to strengthen and heal. Let us hail that powerful name as Edward Perronet did, and crown Him in our heart, "Lord of all."

PRAYER: Heavenly Father, thank you for sending your Son that He might be with us in every experience of life. We rejoice in the thought that He promised to be with us always. May our faith in Him never wane no matter how great the difficulties before us. In Jesus' name, Amen.

THOUGHT: Where Jesus is, hope is always to be found.

2. HOLY, HOLY, HOLY

"The four beasts had each of them six wings . . . and they rest not day and night, saying, Holy, holy, holy, Lord God almighty." (REV. 4:8)

One of the first hymns likely to be sung on Sunday morning is "Holy, Holy, Holy, Lord God Almighty." This hymn lifts our souls in worship and prepares us for the rest of the service. It was written by Reginald Heber (1783-1826) who following a pastorate of many years in England, was made Bishop of Calcutta in 1823. Foreign missions were one of his major interests, so this appointment fulfilled a long-time desire. However, his missionary endeavors were not to last long. Yet during these few years he worked tirelessly, traveling from one appointment to another, always advancing the work of the Church.

Heber had just finished preaching a sermon on the evils of the caste system to a large congregation, and it being a very hot day he decided to return to the house in which he was staying and cool off in the swimming pool. Sometime later his body was found where he had drowned following a stroke.

Heber was a very gifted person and wrote many hymns. "Holy, Holy, Holy," was written to be sung on Trinity Sunday while he was still in his parish in England. After his death his widow published his hymns and poems, and another Anglican rector, John B. Dykes, who was one of England's leading organists, composed the tune to this familiar hymn.

Holy, Holy, Holy! Lord God Almighty!
Early in the morning our song shall rise to Thee;
Holy, Holy, Holy! Merciful and mighty!
God in three persons, blessed Trinity!

* * * * * * *

A traveling salesman who had spent many years in and out of hotels, once visited one that intrigued him. He was amazed by the efficient manner in which it was operated. He was warmly welcomed and everything possible was done for his comfort. When he left he expressed his appreciation for the care he had received and asked why they went to so much trouble to make him comfortable. He discovered that the owner gave every member of his staff a card which they were to keep in a place where they could continually refer to it. On the card were these words, "My reputation is in your hands."

In like manner, as children of God, His reputation is in our hands. The first petition of the Lord's prayer underlines that fact. "Our Father, which art in Heaven, hallowed be Thy name." God's reputation is in our hands. It is our responsibility to keep His name holy. Whenever we degrade God's name, we degrade Him.

PRAYER: Our Father, make us aware of the unlimited power available to us, your children. As we yield ourselves unto You, may we become increasingly conscious of our responsibility to our fellow men. In the Master's name, Amen.

THOUGHT: It is God, not tyrants, who holds the world in his hands.

3. COME, THOU FOUNT OF EVERY BLESSING

"The Son of man indeed goeth as it is written of him: but woe to that man by whom the Son of man is betrayed! good were it for that man if he had never been born." (MARK 14:21)

He didn't like being a barber although there was nothing he could do about it. His father died when he was eight years old and left the family almost penniless. At fourteen he was apprenticed to a London barber, but was never really happy. His unhappiness led him to associate with evil companions whom he thought were always having a good time. His life had been hard and drab since his father's death and working at a job he disliked didn't help matters. Eventually he became like his friends, wild and reckless.

Time passed and the thrill he once received from doing unlawful things began to fade. The early Methodist movement was growing rapidly so he decided it would still be fun to heckle these deluded people. That was a popular pastime with many and he didn't consider it an evil. On their way he and his companions went seeking for such a group to disturb. They selected an open air meeting led by George Whitfield. As they awaited an opportunity to disturb the gathering, the famous evangelist began to preach. His powerful voice could be heard in every direction as he preached on the wrath to come.

As this 17-year-old youth, Robert Robinson (1735-1790) listened, he became frightened. All the sins of his short wild life came before him as the preacher warned his audience to flee from the destruction that would come to the sinful. He felt the evangelist was speaking to him, and repenting of his sins, he decided that from then on he would live a righteous, Christian life. At twenty he came under the influence of John Wesley, and not long after was preaching in one of Wesley's chapels. Three years later, while thinking of the happiness that was his since his conversion he wrote, "Come, Thou Fount of Every Blessing."

Come, thou Fount of every blessing
  Tune my heart to sing thy grace;
Streams of mercy, never ceasing,
  Call for songs of loudest praise.
Teach me some melodious sonnet,
  Sung by flaming tongues above;
Praise the mount! I'm fixed upon it,
  Mount of thy redeeming love.

* * * * * * *

A most unforgettable sermon came on our first visit to the Luray Caverns. After following our guide for nearly an hour, he announced that we had reached the lowest point. He then added jokingly, "You had better be careful of your guide because if he is the wrong one, each step you take will eventually lead to the bottom." In a very real sense this applied to Robert Robinson. He was actually one of the best endowed young men of his day, and God was angling for him, but he continued to allow his recklessness to lead him to a much lower depth. Then he met Jesus through one of His disciples of that day, George Whitfield, and he became a new creature.

PRAYER: Our Father, we have often been foolish. We have taken our way and called it Your way. We pray that You will reclothe us in our rightful mind that we may see ourselves as You see us. This we ask in the name of Your Son. Amen.

THOUGHT: The garment of righteousness is never out of date.

4. STILL, STILL WITH THEE

"My voice shalt thou hear in the morning, O Lord; in the morning will I direct my prayer unto thee." (PSALM 5:3)

Harriet Beecher Stowe (1812-1896) was never a person of affluence; even when fame came to her she never rose far above the poverty level. One reason was that she seemed unable to save her money or invest it properly. Another was that she trusted everyone, and was often imposed upon.

She was not entirely reconciled to the Calvinistic theology of that day. It disturbed her because she liked the more liberal ideas that were emerging. When she was thirteen her father preached a sermon on the love of Christ that touched her deeply. After returning home she entered his study, put her arms around him and said, "Father, I have given myself to Jesus, and he has taken me." That experience never left her though she had a struggle to keep this simple faith. A few years later love became her gospel, and she practiced that love the remainder of her life.

At the age of twenty-five she married a professor, but he had no greater business sense than she. Once he predicted that they would spend their last days in the poorhouse. In a letter to a friend she described her husband in these words, "I was married when I was twenty-five years of age to a man rich in Greek and Hebrew, Latin and Arabic, and, alas! rich in nothing else."

In 1855 her brother, Henry Ward Beecher, asked her to write a hymn for the book, "Plymouth Collection" of hymns he was preparing. The result was this lovely morning hymn of worship, "Still, Still with Thee." The music is from Mendelssohn.

Still, still with thee, when purple morning breaketh,
  When the bird waketh and the shadows flee;
Fairer than morning, lovelier than daylight,
  Dawns the sweet consciousness, I am with thee.

* * * * * * *

In the spring of 1940 Clare Booth made a tour of Europe, interviewing leaders and surveying the conditions in the countries at war. In her book, "Europe in the Spring," she writes, "As a matter of fact, I never heard anybody important really talk seriously about God in Europe in the Spring. But the Sunday after the invasion, all the politicians in Paris went with the people to Notre Dame and prayed on their knees to God to save France for them." That is man's difficulty. His faith in God is great when the invasion is on, but in the Spring, when there is no danger, God is forgotten. If one's God is no bigger than that, his songs will never rise to the Eternal early in the morning.

PRAYER: Help us to remember Your claim on our lives, O Lord, that we may be always ready to do your will. In Jesus' name. Amen.

THOUGHT: Do we thank God in the morning for the strength we will receive during the day?

5. GUIDE ME, O THOU GREAT JEHOVAH

"Thou shalt guide me with thy counsel, and afterwards receive me to glory." (PSALM 72:24)

This hymn seeking God's guidance was written by an outstanding Welsh itinerant Methodist preacher, who studied to be a doctor. For forty years, William Williams (1717-1791) traveled a wide circuit preaching and singing the gospel. He was called the Watts of Wales, having authored during that time over 800 hymns, the best known being the hymn of this meditation. Yet we might not have had this inspirational song were it not for Lady Huntington. She read one of William's books and asked him to prepare a collection of hymns to be used in George Whitefield's Orphans House in America. This hymn appeared in that collection. It was translated from the Welsh by Rev. Peter Williams, a contemporary of William. The trouble was, Peter took certain liberties with some of the verses, changing phrases to suit his taste. Of this we can be sure: the first verse belongs to William Williams and many of the remaining verses also.

Guide me, O Thou great Jehovah,
Pilgrim through this barren land;
I am weak, but Thou art mighty;
Hold me with Thy powerful hand.
Bread of Heaven, Bread of Heaven,
Feed me till I want no more,
Feed me till I want no more.

* * * * * * *

Sam Higginbottom, a pioneer agricultural missionary to India said that when he was a boy in England, a great misfortune overtook the family and they were forced to move into a slum area. The boy could look from his window and see the many saloons in the neighborhood. He watched little ragged children begging money from drunken fathers to buy bread, or wives receiving curses and blows for much the same reason. It was then he made a vow never to drink. That was God guiding him and that experience was far more convincing than the loudest voice man could use.

Such an experience might have happened to us and we were probably not aware of the fact that this was God seeking us. He was guiding us by offering the bread of life we needed. It is one thing to sing about the guidance of God. Anyone with a voice can do that. It is another thing, however, to recognize that God is seeking us through the hymns we sing. He is always guiding us in many of the events we take for granted, but we are often unaware of both His presence and His desire for a change in our life.

PRAYER: Guide me, O Thou great Jehovah,
Pilgrim through this barren land;
I am weak, but Thou art mighty;
Hold me with Thy powerful hand. Amen.

THOUGHT: No one can live right without God to guide him.

6. PRAISE GOD FROM WHOM ALL BLESSINGS FLOW

"Praise ye the Lord, O give thanks unto the Lord; for He is good; for his mercy endureth forever." (PSALM 106:1)

Our doxology was written by a man who defied his king, yet was made bishop. Thomas Ken (1637-1711) intended these words for morning, noon and evening prayer for his students at Oxford. In his earlier ministry, Ken had refused lodging to Nell Gwynn, King Charles' mistress. Yet when the office of Bishop opened the king said, "Give it to the little man who refused poor Nell lodging."

This was not the only time Ken offended Charles II. He constantly reminded the king that he must renounce his sins. Charles cringed every time Ken preached. The dissipated monarch used to say, "I must go hear Ken tell me all my faults." It is said that the bishop had the voice of a nightingale, which could be one reason Charles liked to listen to his sermons.

Ken later displeased another monarch, William III, who deprived him of his office and caused him to retire in poverty. Through the kindness of a friend, however, Ken was given a home where he spent the final years of his life in peace. His request before his death was that he be carried to his grave "by six of the poorest men in the parish."

Praise God from whom all blessings flow,
Praise Him, all creatures here below,
Praise Him above, ye heavenly hosts:
Praise Father, Son, and Holy Ghost.

* * * * * * *

Praise the Lord! We hear this expression more today than perhaps at any time since the day of the apostles. This is not emotionalism. It is as it should be. We are not ashamed to sing hymns of praise in church, such as the doxology. But why reserve our praise for hymns? Why not let ourselves go and continually shout our praises to God? We will feel better every time we do, for we are the children of God. Let us remember this every time we walk down the street, and in every plan we make. That should cause us to burst into words of praise. May we say repeatedly, "I am a child of God and because of this I must live as He expects me to." May we add to every desire of our heart, praises to the One who gave us voices to sing.

PRAYER: We praise your name, O God, because you are worthy to be praised. It is you who made us and sent Jesus to redeem us. Forgive us when we shout ourselves hoarse at sports events and remain glum and silent before the greatest event the world has ever known. In Jesus' name. Amen.

THOUGHT: The most thankful people are usually those who have passed through the deepest waters. They have discovered the healing balm of praise.

7. GOD OF OUR FATHERS, KNOWN OF OLD

"Hast thou not known? hast thou not heard, that the everlasting God, the Lord, the Creator of the ends of the earth, fainteth not, neither is weary? there is no searching in his understanding." (ISAIAH 40:28)

He had been working on his project for days. Scraps of paper on which he had already written surrounded him. He read them over repeatedly but to his usually keen mind they were nothing but words.

The Jubilee of Queen Victoria's reign was approaching and Rudyard Kipling (1865-1936) had been asked by the *London Times* to prepare a poem for the occasion. The due date had already arrived but all he had to show for his effort were scraps of paper. The *Times* was not happy by his long delay in responding. They began to bombard him with letters, but his answers were always the same. His poem was not ready. Next he began receiving telegrams from them and he knew something had to be done. He shut himself in a room determined to stay there until the poem was finished.

Shutting himself in a room might not have worked immediately but it proved to be the answer. "I searched through those dozens of sketches," he said, "till at last I found just one line I liked. That was, "Lest we forget!" Around those words the Recessional was written." He gave a sigh of relief upon its completion and later said, "That poem gave me more trouble than anything I ever wrote."

God of our fathers, known of old,
Lord of our far flung battle line,
Beneath whose awful hand we hold
Dominion over palm and pine;
Lord God of Hosts, be with us yet,
Lest we forget, lest we forget!

* * * * * * *

Over a hundred years ago, Bishop Whipple, an apostle to the Indians, listened to the words of an Indian who traveled many miles to see him. "I was once a wild man," he said, "living beyond the Turtle Mountains. I knew that my people were perishing. I never looked in the face of my child that my heart was not sick. My father told me that there was a great spirit and I have often gone to the woods and tried to ask him for help, but all I received was the sound of my own voice."

It was then the Indian looked sadly in the face of the Bishop and said, "You do not know what I mean. You have never stood in the dark, reached out your hand and took hold of nothing."

What a tragedy it is if in the hour of our pain and sorrow we reach out our hand and take hold of nothing. It is a sign we have too long left God out of our life. This not only applies to a nation but also to an individual. An emergency situation is no time to go searching for a God we have neglected.

PRAYER: Lord God of Hosts, be with us yet,
Lest we forget, lest we forget. Amen.

THOUGHT: God has dealt bountifully with us. May we deal as bountifully with Him.

8. GOD MOVES IN A MYSTERIOUS WAY

"O the depth of the riches both of the wisdom and knowledge of God! How unsearchable are his judgements, and his ways are past finding out!" (Romans 11:33)

God does seem to move in mysterious ways and no one was more aware of that than William Cowper (1731-1800). Cowper was a Church of England layman, who studied law but soon grew to dislike the profession and turned his attention towards literature. In this he excelled even though his periods of despondency kept his work at a minimum. His instability began when he was to take an examination for a clerkship in the House of Lords, and he dreaded that ordeal so that it produced a severe mental breakdown. He wrote poetry and prose and was considered one of the best letter writers in all literature.

During the long periods of melancholy he tried to commit suicide. He lived through a dose of laudanum that would have killed another. Failing in that he took a knife from its place of concealment but he could not thrust it into his body. He attempted to hang himself but the material he used broke. This was followed by a long stay in an asylum. His later attempt to drown himself in the river Ouse likewise ended in failure.

One of the great mysteries to Cowper was why he always failed in his attempts at self-destruction when others who used the same means succeeded. Why would the Lord continue to keep alive one who possessed his mental malady? He wondered about this and it led to the writing of the hymn, "God moves in a mysterious way His wonders to perform". Perhaps the ways of God are not as mysterious as Cowper thought for God knew that this man's pious writings and hymns would lead countless souls to Jesus, His Son.

God moves in a mysterious way
His wonders to perform;
He plants his footsteps in the sea,
And rides upon the storm.

* * * * * * *

I will never forget the first time I saw my dear mother cry. At the time I thought she was foolish and old fashioned for I was in my middle teens and quite independent. Her tears were because she found a package of cigarettes in my pocket, and she didn't want her boy to smoke. It broke her heart because she had other plans for me. I didn't know what those plans were at the time but I did a few years later when I came home and said, "I was converted tonight and I am going into the ministry". Her eyes became misty again, but they were not tears of sorrow, but tears of joy. As I look back now I realize how God was moving in the mysterious way Cowper wrote about, but this time it was through my mother. My decision to enter the ministry was an answer to her prayers.

What led to my decision? An incident that happened a few nights before. I was president of an athletic club that used the gym of our large city church. The time came when the church was to conduct revival services with an outside evangelist. These services were held the same week we were to have our most important basketball game and it required practicing every night. The assistant pastor came to me and practically demanded that both the practice and the game be postponed that week, and that our club attend the services instead. He was not very tactful and neither was I. We both became angry and I decided against everything he suggested. It was not long before my conscience began to bother me and I persuaded the fellows to give up one night of practice and attend the service instead. That was God moving in a mysterious way again, for that was the night I was converted.

PRAYER: Our Father, when faith grows dim will you provide the light needed to see through the darkness that surrounds us? In that light shall we see light and know the meaning of the difficult experience through which we have passed. In Jesus' name. Amen.

THOUGHT: Life was never meant to be lived without Jesus.

9. HOW GREAT THOU ART

"The heavens declare the glory of God; and the firmament showeth his handiwork." (PSALM 19:1)

The young Swedish minister was deep in thought thinking about God. The beauty of God's handiwork completely surrounded him. He was hiking through the woods admiring the trees and flowers, the shimmering lake and the green meadows after the passing of a thunderstorm. The greatness of God's mighty work in nature caused the twenty-six year old pastor, Carl Boberg (1859-1940) to write a poem in praise of the One who created all this beauty and of Jesus who gave his life for the salvation of the world.

The poem he called "O, Great God," and it was published in several periodicals and then seemingly forgotten. In the meantime Boberg went about his work of preaching the Gospel and serving the needs of those under his care. For fifteen years he served as a senator in the Swedish parliament, also using his talents as a religious editor. Though he might have forgotten his poem, it did not remain dormant. It was discovered and published in Polish, German and Russian as a hymn.

Later the poem was published in English under the title "O Mighty God," but was rarely sung and almost forgotten once more. It was resurrected by an English missionary, Rev. Stuart K. Hine. While in his mission field the Russian version of the hymn came to his attention. Hine was unaware of its authorship and thought a Russian prisoner had written it. It impressed him so much that he translated it into English, giving it the title, "How Great Thou Art."

Hine had an experience similar to that of the original author. The first verse was completed after a thunderstorm in the Carpathian mountains that caused him to seek shelter for the night. The second stanza of his English version came after a group of young Christians played and sang the Russian words in the woods and forest glades of Romania. The music, a popular Swedish folk song, is well known throughout Europe. The second stanza follows:

> When through the woods and forest glades I wander
> And hear the birds sing sweetly in the trees,
> When I look down from lofty mountain grandeur,
> And hear the brook and feel the gentle breeze,

* * * * * * *

On numerous occasions I have come face to face with God in the same way. Never will I forget that fall day when I looked down from the top of Mount Mooselauke in northern New Hampshire, and saw the lakes and villages below and the surrounding mountains in the distance. That in itself brought God near, but this was a day when the color of the leaves was at its height. Every possible shade of yellow and red mingled with the green of the evergreens, and as I looked upon the scene I knew that no human hand could adequately paint that picture, nor words do it justice. It was not only a riot of color, but it was God. The only thing I could do was to pray. I knew then why the Bible calls the man who said in his heart, "There is no

God," a fool. No one could stand on that mountain top that day and say, "There is no God."

No one can find God unless he is going God's way. If you have taken the wrong road, reverse your direction, look in the face of Jesus, and you will see God. Then you will recognize Him in every created thing before you.

PRAYER: We would incline our ears, O Lord, to your voice. Speak through the beauty of each day and night. May we not only hear your voice but see your handiwork in every mountain, stream and forest, and in the little bird that nests in your trees. In Jesus' name. Amen.

THOUGHT: God is not very real to one who cannot see Him in nature.

10. SAFELY THROUGH ANOTHER WEEK

"This is the day that the Lord hath made; we will rejoice and be glad in it." (PSALM 118:24)

Early in the year 1400 Thomas a'Kempis, a pious monk who spent much of his time copying the Bible and other religious works, wrote a book entitled "Imitation of Christ." John Wesley was intrigued by this mystical writer and kept his book always in easy reach. Three hundred years after "Imitation of Christ" appeared, it fell into the hands of a very profane slave-ship captain. To idle away his time he decided to see what it contained.

He said, "I carelessly took up Stanhope's Thomas a'Kempis as I had often done before, to pass away the time. However, while I was reading this time an involuntary suggestion arose in my mind. What if these things should be true?" His conscience bothered him for a while, but he soon put what he read out of his mind and went on as thoughtlessly as before. That night there arose a violent storm, and the one thing that seemed to fill his mind was the Christ that a'Kempis portrayed so effectively. As a result, John Newton (1725-1807) gave his heart to the Lord, promising that he would leave the slave trade and become a minister. That promise at sea was later fulfilled, and he not only became a preacher but a hymn writer as well. In a quiet moment as he meditated on the dangers that once faced him at sea and the peace and contentment that was now his, Newton began to write a hymn of thanksgiving for God's guidance from Sabbath to Sabbath. With that guidance he expressed the joy that came with worship.

Safely through another week
God has brought us on our way;
Let us now a blessing seek
Waiting in His courts today;
Day of all the week the best,
Emblem of eternal rest;
Day of all the week the best,
Emblem of eternal rest.

* * * * * * *

What is on our mind when we think of the coming Sabbath? Are we thrilled with entering the House of God for worship? Or is our mind on lesser things that can be accomplished any day of the week?

May nothing but illness or an emergency prevent us from worshipping in the Lord's House each week, for it is there miracles happen. It is there with a sincere heart that we can thank Him for His many blessings and His protecting care since we last met. It is there we can bring Him our needs and the names of others who face difficult situations. It is in His Church that we can dedicate our lives anew to Him and to the work for which we are called. Let us thank God for leading us safely through another week.

PRAYER: Lord, thank you for the Sabbath Day, when we can gather the necessary strength for the week before us. In Jesus' name. Amen.

THOUGHT: Jesus has every vital vitamin necessary for our spiritual health, including worship, and they are as potent now as in His day.

11. SUN OF MY SOUL

"Then shall the righteous shine forth as the sun in the kingdom of their Father." (MATT. 13:43)

Many hymns are written following a tragic experience or after a great soul changing event. Others are meant to inspire those who are seeking a better way of life. "Sun of My Soul, Thou Savior Dear," was one of the latter. The Rev. John Keble (1792-1866) who wrote the words was a deeply spiritual Church of England clergyman in an age when many were indifferent to the call of God. He really never expected his poem to be a hymn. It was written to inspire others to a more devout Christian life. He inserted it with other devotional material in his book called "The Christian Year."

Another characteristic of this good man was that he had no intention of seeking advancement in the church, although he was well trained for any position offered him. After his ordination he settled in a small town where he became pastor of three struggling churches at a salary of about an hundred pounds a year. There he remained throughout his active ministry, fulfilling his pastoral duties and spending much time in writing. It was here he wrote his hymns and found peace and happiness. Although he had ample opportunity for advancement, a larger church or a greater salary never tempted him.

Sun of my soul, thou Savior dear,
It is not night if thou be near;
O may no earth-born cloud arise
To hide thee from thy servant's eyes.

* * * * * * *

Who walks with us in our lonely hours? This I know; there is not a pew in our church on any Sunday that does not contain at least one lonely person. That loneliness can come through sorrow, suffering, misunderstanding, a lingering illness or concern for a loved one. Are we able to see that person? Is there enough of Christ in us to help make that discovery? If we should be that lonely person, would we be aware of the One who is walking by our side?

If not, then who is giving us strength to face our lonely days and nights? If it is not Jesus then our loneliness and despair will not soon end. We need Jesus in every experience of life. He is the One who has the message and assurance we need. He is the Sun that

John Keble was writing about. Who else will light our way in the darkness or give us hope when the storms of life engulf us? Earth-born clouds are bound to arise but none will ever be big enough to hide Jesus from our eyes.

PRAYER: Our lives are in darkness without you, O Christ. You are the Sun of our soul and we need you every hour. Draw near to us in our loneliness and forgive us when we seek help from every other source, and seek You as a last resort. In your dear name. Amen.

THOUGHT: Jesus can give a new glow to our life.

12. WHEN ALL THY MERCIES, O MY GOD

"And there arose a great storm of wind, and the waves beat into the ship, so that it was now full." (MARK 4:37)

Numerous hymns have been written by those devout souls who felt that only the hand of God saved them from certain destruction. One such was the celebrated English poet and essayist, Joseph Addison (1672-1719). Addison was the best English writer of his day, and never forgot his religious training as a boy. Today he would be called "a preacher's kid". His father, Lancelot Addison, was the rector of Milston, Wiltshire, and Joseph was born in the rectory, May 1, 1672. He was educated at Oxford and excelled in poetry, both Latin and English.

This hymn and another, "How Are Thy Servants Blest, O Lord," were written as the result of a violent storm at sea. The ship upon which Addison was a passenger was caught in this dangerous storm off the coast of Genoa, Italy, in 1701. Shipwreck seemed imminent and almost all on board prepared for the worst. However, the frail craft survived and though many forgot this near disaster in the months ahead, Addison did not. Lord Macaulay, commenting on this experience said that even the captain gave up all hope of saving his vessel. While terror filled the hearts and minds of those on board, Addison began to meditate on God. His thoughts were filled with the goodness and mercy of the Eternal, and when the storm subsided and the ship made shore, this English poet wrote his two hymns of thanksgiving to God for guiding them through the treacherous waters to safety. He was never ashamed of his faith and included all his hymns in the "Spectator" for all to see.

When all thy mercies, O my God,
My rising soul surveys,
Transported with the view, I'm lost
In wonder, love, and praise.

* * * * * * *

Are we really thankful people? Do we thank Him for the sun that warms us or the rain that refreshes? Do we thank Him for the moonlight, starry nights or the beautiful cloudless days? How often do we thank Him for loved ones who minister to us and friends who help us when a need arises? If we fail to give thanks for these daily blessings, we would hardly be in the spirit to thank Him for saving us from life's disasters. Joseph Addison was so thankful for the mercy of God that he was forced to write about it and to keep repeating it continually.

If God has enabled us to escape the tragedies of life, let us rejoice and give thanks. As many blessings come wrapped in the package labeled "what didn't happen," as in the one revealing what did take place. Let us give thanks!

PRAYER: Jesus, Saviour, pilot me
Over life's tempestuous sea.
Unknown waves before me roll,
Hiding rock and treacherous shoal;
Chart and compass come from thee:
Jesus, Saviour, pilot me. Amen.

THOUGHT: Let us be thankful for the opportunity of saying "thank you" to God.

13. LEAD KINDLY LIGHT

"As long as I am in the world, I am the light of the world." (JOHN 9:5)

The heart of the thirty-two year old Anglican clergyman was heavy. For some time he had deplored the lack of spiritual vitality within his denomination. The Church of Rome seemed to possess what he desired, therefore he had left England for a visit to the Vatican. He discussed the problem with the leaders of the Catholic Church. They sympathized with him and tried to help him. However, he left their presence a very disturbed man. To make matters worse, he became seriously ill while trying to comfort victims of an epidemic near Sicily. For days he lay near death, during which time he wondered about God's plan for his life.

It was a month before he could think about returning to England, and then he faced another problem: he would have to wait three weeks for a boat from Palermo. His problems were many, but they were not yet over. He was as anxious now to get home as he had been earlier to leave England in search of the answers that would give him peace of mind. However, in the Mediterranean Sea, the wind dropped and his boat was becalmed. Restlessly he paced the deck, always asking, "When are we going to sail?"

It was during this time of waiting that the meaning of all that had happened seemed to make sense to John Henry Newman (1801-1890). He opened his Bible and read again the references to the leadership of God. It was night. The light of the star that was to guide the captain when the wind would again arise, was twinkling above him. If so small a light could guide the captain, surely Jesus, the Light of the world, could guide him. With a peace he had not experienced before, Newman wrote:

Lead kindly Light, amid the encircling gloom,
Lead Thou me on!
The night is dark, and I am far from home,
Lead Thou me on!
Keep Thou my feet; I do not ask to see
The distant scene; one step enough for me.

* * * * * * *

I was seated outside one of our large hospitals when a small boy approached, sobbing. "What's wrong?" I asked. His reply was, "I'm lost." I asked what street he wanted, then pointed out the direction. Tears began again as he said, "Mister, maybe I won't find it. Won't you walk with me!"

It is a horrible feeling to be lost, and that day we were both on unfamiliar ground. The boy had lost his way home, and I was trying to work my way out of the seemingly unbelievable experience that a loved one was soon to depart. So, hand in hand, each silently comforting the other, we walked to the boy's home.

John Henry Newman knew exactly where he was going when he

went to Rome, but to a certain extent he was lost. He was unsure of the direction in which he should go. He needed someone to lead him.

If at this moment you are not sure of the direction in which you must go, it is a sign you need a guide. You will need more than one to point the way: you will need someone to walk with you, and that someone is Jesus.

PRAYER: Lead, kindly Light; lead Thou me on. In the name of Jesus, the Light of the World. Amen.

THOUGHT: If the Lord is with me, what have I to fear?

14. GOD WILL TAKE CARE OF YOU

"He shall cover thee with his feathers, and under his wings shalt thou trust; his truth shall be thy shield and buckler." (PSALM 91:4)

Rev. and Mrs. W. L. Stillman Martin and their small son were visiting friends in New York state. While there, Mr. Martin was asked to preach at a local church. Sunday morning arrived and Mrs. Martin, who had been ill during the visit, suddenly became worse. Her husband was about to cancel the invitation when the son said, "Father, if God wants you to preach, won't He take care of mother while you're away?" That seemed to be God's voice speaking to the minister, so he gathered what was necessary and hurried to the church. On his return his son handed him a piece of paper, on which his wife, Civilla D. Martin (1869-1948) had written the poem "God Will Take Care of You." Despite her illness, the words of her young son were so precious that she spent the hour writing this poem based on them. Her evangelist husband set the words to music and sang them as she listened from her sick bed.

"Be not dismayed, what'er betide,
God will take care of you;
Beneath His wings of love abide,
God will take care of you.

God will take care of you
Through ev'ry day, o'er all the way;
He will take care of you,
God will take care of you."

* * * * * * *

Victor Hugo once wrote to his little girl from the sea shore, telling her that he had walked on the beach and had written her name in the sand. "Tonight," he wrote, "the rising tide will erase it, but nothing can ever erase your name from your father's heart." So it is with us. The tides may sweep over us and cause us to be dismayed because much that we cherish has been taken from us, but we are still precious in the sight of God and He will take care of our needs. No tide, however vicious, can erase our names from the Father's heart.

PRAYER: Thank you heavenly Father, for the blessings that have come to us through your Son. He who stilled the storms of his day we call upon to still the raging storms of our generation. In His name. Amen.

THOUGHT: God knows all about you and your needs. Trust Him for the answer.

15. O LITTLE TOWN OF BETHLEHEM

"Unto you is born this day in the city of David a Saviour, which is Christ the Lord." (LUKE 2:11)

The Church of the Holy Trinity in Philadelphia was looking for a new rector. Recently it had come to their attention that a young student at a nearby seminary was filling a little mission chapel through his dynamic preaching. He was considered one of the most exciting and inspirational preachers in that area. A committee from the church, after much persuasion, reluctantly decided that they should, at least, go and hear him.

While waiting for the young man to appear, their attention was drawn to a tall beardless youth taking a short cut to the chapel. He was apparently late and in a hurry, as he waded through a stream, vaulted over a fence, and finally reached his destination. If that was a surprise his next move came as a shock. Wiping off his clothes and brushing back his hair he took his place behind the pulpit.

Can this possibly be Phillips Brooks (1835-1893) whom they came to hear, they asked each other? As they were ready to leave the voice of the young preacher compelled them to stay. It wasn't long before his effective and spiritual message so gripped them that they knew this was the young man the church needed. When they left they said, "Don't you accept another appointment until you hear from us." It wasn't long before he received a call to become their rector.

Three years later his church thought so much of him that he was sent abroad for a year. While in the Holy Land he traced the footsteps of the Master. That Christmas he was in Bethlehem. The impression of that Christmas eve never left him and two years later he wrote for the children of his church these beautiful words based on his Bethlehem experience.

O little town of Bethlehem,
How still we see thee lie!
Above thy deep and dreamless sleep
The silent stars go by;
Yet in thy dark streets shineth
The everlasting light;
The hopes and fears of all the years
Are met in thee tonight.

* * * * * * *

What will we get this Christmas? Will we get a new heart? As our physical heart so often needs attention, so does the heart of our spiritual life. Only Jesus can give us that renewal, and He is the heart of Christmas. That suggests that we must spend much time with Him if December 25th will have the meaning it should for us.

How many hours will we spend in Bible reading, meditation and prayer? Surely we cannot come to Christmas prepared if we miss these means of spiritual growth.

How regular will be our church attendance? The church can tell us how to get a new heart. The church has the message we need, not only for our life but for our day. If the medical profession can help us get rid of our body aches, the church can help us to overcome our heartaches.

What we get this year for Christmas that will be all important, will not come in glittering packages but rather through the One who came to give His life a ransom for many.

PRAYER: We have many things for which to be thankful, O Lord, but the greatest of them all is a Saviour. May we gladly accept Jesus today. In Jesus' name. Amen.

THOUGHT: Christmas is a story of love, and love is a story that never grows old.

16. IN THE CROSS OF CHRIST I GLORY

"God forbid that I should glory, save in the cross of our Lord Jesus Christ." (GALATIANS 6:14)

Sir John Bowring (1792-1872) was a statesman who exerted a tremendous influence upon his generation. He was able to speak thirteen languages and dialects – some sources say even more. As a result he was given consular appointments in seven different capitals by his government. While Governor of Hong Kong he helped to fix the opium traffic on China. He was so hated in that crown colony that an attempt was made on his life. Arsenic was put in the food prepared for his breakfast. His wife later died from the effects of this poisoning and he became seriously ill.

Among his many accomplishments were his religious essays and hymns. His most popular hymn is, "In the Cross of Christ I Glory," which is sung with great feeling by Christians everywhere. The Christians of China were slow in accepting the hymn because of his connection with the opium trade. There is one thing to remember, however, that this hymn was written while he was still an idealistic youth in his early thirties and before he became corrupted by the great power placed in his hands. We must not think of the mistakes he made when we sing this hymn, but instead remember that as a youth he wanted to be a preacher.

In the cross of Christ I glory,
Towering o'er the wrecks of time;
All the light of sacred story
Gathers round its head sublime.

* * * * * * *

The wearing of the cross has often been made a common and sometimes cheap thing. This was brought to my attention not long ago, when in a prominent place in our newspaper appeared a picture of several young women arrested in a vice raid, yet dangling from the neck of each was a cross.

I wear a cross. I shall continue to do so, but my conscience will be ill at ease until I measure up to its standards. The cross is a constant reminder of Jesus and His sacrifice. It stands as an emblem of our Christian faith. If by way of His cross we have become fresh and clean again, we can safely wear it and never be ashamed.

PRAYER: Heavenly Father, we pray that our future will not

have a cross in it. If one should be there, give us the courage to accept it as your Son did. In Jesus' name. Amen.

THOUGHT: Jesus urged his followers to take a cross, not wait for one.

17. JESUS, I MY CROSS HAVE TAKEN

"He that taketh not his cross, and followeth not after Me is not worthy of Me." (MATT. 10:38)

How often we have heard preachers quote the words of Isaiah, "the weak take the prey." The accomplishments of the weak in literature is astounding. This is likewise true in hymnology. Some of our finest hymns were written by devout souls with weak bodies. Henry Francis Lyte (1793-1849) who wrote "Abide with Me," is one of those. He also wrote other poems, among them the hymn poem, "Jesus I My Cross Have Taken." Lyte had a keen mind but never a strong body. He was left an orphan when a child and he could never forget the struggle that was his in getting an education. In spite of poverty and a weak constitution he eventually graduated from Trinity College, Dublin, and at twenty-one became pastor of a small Anglican church.

It is said he possessed a face that was of feminine beauty, but that did not deter him from his desire to do everything possible for the Master. He didn't want to be known as one who lived and died without any real accomplishments. For this reason he worked hard in his parish when other men with his weak body would have given up. All his mature life he was aware of tuberculosis, but he kept his mind continually upon his work. He eventually married an heiress and was later transferred to Lower Brixham in Devonshire, where for twenty-four years he gave himself in loving service. It was while in this parish that he wrote his own spiritual autobiography in the words of the hymn for this meditation. The hymn is usually sung to the tune "Ellesdie" composed by Mozart.

Jesus, I my cross have taken
  All to leave and follow Thee;
Destitute, despised, forsaken,
  Thou, from hence, my all shalt be.

Perish every fond ambition,
  All I've sought, or hoped, or known;
Yet how rich is my condition;
  God and heaven are still my own!

* * * * * * *

HIS CROSS – MY CROSS

His cross was heavy, awkward, large,
  So very plain;
Designed to cause the utmost sense
  Of human pain.

My cross is made of yellow gold,
  A pretty thing;
I wear it, yet it has no weight,
  Or painful sting.

His cross bloomed from the blood-sweat of
  Gethsemane.
And bore salvation through the heat
  Of Calvary.

My cross has never felt the drip
  Of blood and sweat,
And not through choice or force has it
  And Calvary met.

His cross still sheds upon the world
  A deathless glow;
My cross just dangles from a chain,
  Exposed for show.

G.W.W.

PRAYER: Our Father, as we look upon Calvary we realize the depth of concern and love it reveals. Help us to understand that this sacrifice was for us, and may it lead to a renewed dedication of our lives to You and your Son. Amen.

THOUGHT: We are expected to do more than wear a cross. We are to take up the cross and follow Jesus.

18. BEHOLD THE SAVIOR OF MANKIND

"When they were come to the place, which is called Calvary, there they crucified him." (LUKE 23:33)

He was a pious man, a faithful pastor, scholar, poet, politician, independent thinker and very opinionated. He was also loyal to King William III, and regularly prayed God's protection and divine blessing upon him. His wife did not share that loyalty and refused to say "amen" at the end of that petition in his morning prayer. Finally, her refusal became too much for him so he said, "Sukey, if we are to have two kings we must have two beds." With that he began sleeping in another bed, eventually leaving their home for London. There he stayed until King William died and the cause of friction between him and his wife was removed.

Yet, in spite of this incident, he loved his wife and family. He was always poor for his salary was not sufficient to feed and clothe his ten living children. Of nineteen born to them, nine had died in infancy. He was in debt most of his life and was well acquainted with debtor's prison. His incarceration came as a surprise but he was not long dismayed. The way in which it happened, however, was both cruel and shocking. He was arrested in his church yard after conducting a service of baptism. His adversary came after the money he had borrowed sometime before and which, of course, he was unable to pay. As a result he was jailed for four months, and were it not for the financial help of a few friends and the influence of the Duke of Buckingham, his stay in prison could have been much longer.

Four years later the parsonage at Epworth caught fire and Samuel Wesley Sr. (1662-1735) stood in agony below, because his son John was left sleeping in the upstairs bedroom. The boy was eventually saved when a tall man stood on the shoulders of another and John fell into his arms. With tears in his eyes Samuel said, "Thank God! My children are safe, let the house go!"

Something else came to life as the result of that fire. A sudden draft of wind blew a piece of paper from the house to the rectory garden. It was later picked up to be discarded when it was discovered to be a manuscript of the hymn, "Behold the Saviour of Mankind" that Samuel had written some time before.

Behold the Saviour of Mankind
Nailed to the shameful tree!

How vast the love that him inclined
To bleed and die for thee!

* * * * * * *

Studert Kennedy repeatedly shocked his hearers by the way in which he presented gospel truths. The one thing he wrote that aroused his readers as effectively as anything he said, was a poem called "Indifference." He explained how through indifference, caused by a lost vision, the Master was cruelly crucified. He then shifts the scene to his modern day England and pictured Jesus walking those fog shrouded and rain swept streets. No longer did anyone yell, "Crucify," or even put a hand on him. They ignored Him, not even glancing in His direction. "They never hurt a hair of Him," the poet continued, "they only let Him die." The scene is clear, people hastening by Him on the street, leaving Him in the rain. The poem ends with these words, "And Jesus crouched against a wall – and cried for Calvary." He would rather be crucified than ignored.

As I view that scene I ask myself the question, "Am I shoving Jesus to Calvary through indifference? Am I ignoring Him? Even though my voice might utter no words, is my heart saying, 'Let Him be crucified?' " God forbid that this should be true of anyone calling himself a Christian.

PRAYER: We realize, our Father, that the Christian life is worth any sacrifice it might cost. May we be willing to pay the price in our day that the disciples did in theirs. In Jesus' name. Amen.

THOUGHT: Christianity without a cross is worth exactly what it cost – nothing.

19. INTO THE WOODS MY MASTER WENT

"Then cometh Jesus with them unto a place called Gethsemane, and sayeth unto the disciples, Sit ye here while I go and pray yonder." (MATT. 26:36)

He was a dreamer in spite of his disease. They were not daydreams. Rather they were words that formed beautiful poems. The problem was that he usually seemed far away from writing materials. He refused, however, to let his dreams die, so he wrote on torn scraps of paper, the backs of envelopes, musical programs, magazines or whatever was handy at the time. He even wrote when he was too weak to lift food to his mouth.

As a child his first love was music. When still very young he could play the piano and organ, the flute, violin, banjo and guitar. His next great love was poetry. There were times when he was never sure which came first. He graduated from Oglethorpe College in 1860 with high honors and remained there as a tutor. Then came the Civil War and at nineteen he enlisted as a private in the Confederate army. Three times he refused promotion. After the war he studied law and practiced with his father until 1872.

He was constantly besieged by sickness. It had now become so severe that he traveled to Texas for a change of climate. Not getting any better he settled in Baltimore, but his health continued to deteriorate. There were months when he was unable to work. He again visited several states but no relief came. Sickness and poverty became his lot. He loved his little family and kept writing to support them. His faithful wife stood courageously by his side and supported every move he made. She was not the only courageous one. Sidney Lanier (1842-1881) slowly dying of tuberculosis, kept writing and even lecturing. His last lecture was given when he was too weak to rise, and sitting in a chair he slowly read what he had written. Three months later he died.

He loved nature and as he studied the trees one day when he was trying desperately to keep alive, they seemed to suggest sympathy with Jesus in Gethsemane. Again there came the dream and he wrote the beautiful hymn poem, "Into the Woods My Master Went." When he finished his poem he had only one more year to live.

Into the woods my Master went,
  Clean forspent, forspent;
Into the woods my Master came,
  Forspent with love and shame.
But the olives they were blind to Him,
  The little gray leaves were kind to Him,
The thorn-tree had a mind to Him,
  When into the woods He came.

* * * * * * * *

Unlike Sidney Lanier the citizens of Jerusalem accepted Jesus as king, but their hymns of praise were only superficial. "Blessed is He that cometh in the name of the Lord," they shouted as He passed them on the streets of their city. But that is not a street song. That is a sanctuary song. How many times have you heard that sung in the streets of your city? Never! You heard those words when you were worshipping in a sanctuary.

One of the world's great actresses was discovered weeping after one of her most brilliant performances. Her friend said, "Why, dearest, you ought to be the happiest woman on the stage because you are admired every time you make an appearance." "Oh, Jane," she replied, "My heart longs for something better and surer than this." This was a sanctuary song in a place where street songs are more commonly sung. The Lord was riding in triumph that day in the dressing room of a theater. Is He riding in triumph on the streets of our city and in the aisles of our church?

PRAYER: Our Father, like your Son we too will have Gethsemane experiences in our life. When that hour comes may we possess the same confidence and faith in You that Jesus had and be able to sincerely say, "Thy will be done." In Jesus' name. Amen.

THOUGHT: In the hour of deepest gloom Jesus beheld an unfading light and triumphantly predicted victory.

20. THE OLD RUGGED CROSS

"And when they were come to the place, which is called Calvary, there they crucified him." (LUKE 23:33)

The Methodist minister had difficulty finishing a hymn he had started. In a vision he saw Christ on the cross just as clearly as if looking upon the scene in real life. He wanted a better understanding of this event and he spent much time in prayer and the reading of the Scriptures. The vision was clear enough but the words he sought to describe that scene eluded him. He knew what he wanted to say and even a melody kept coming to his mind, but try as he might he couldn't complete the poem he had started. God seemed to be telling him to wait and finish his hymn later. Therefore he laid the work aside and turned to the many other problems of his parish.

Sometime later, Rev. George Bennard (1873-1958) was invited to conduct evangelistic services in another parish. It was there his vision of the cross was renewed and the problems that were once present vanished. It was then the words of "The Old Rugged Cross" as we know it began to flow from his pen. He had become the author-composer of one of the most beloved hymns of the church.

On a hill far away stood an old rugged cross,
 The emblem of suffering and shame;
And I love that old cross where the dearest and best
 For a world of lost sinners was slain.

* * * * * * *

The church I served in Fort Lauderdale, Florida had a cross at the front extending nearly the height of the building. Lights were so placed behind it that it was not only a thing of beauty but became a showpiece. Pictures were constantly taken of it, and it appeared on covers of magazines, Christmas cards and as an illustration for various articles. Visitors to the city would come at night to photograph it. Our church stationery carried the motto, "Look for the Big Cross."

Our Scripture verse speaks of a big cross too. It was raised on Calvary, and was well publicized. People came from miles around to look at it, but on that early occasion they came to see a man who was to die upon it. In one place the Scripture says, "They stood beholding." They did not come to look at a beautiful cross. They came to look at a crucifixion and they did nothing to save the one who was nailed upon it. They came not to weep but to jeer.

We look upon a big cross also, an old rugged cross. What do we see? What feelings do we have? Do we know what Jesus was giving His life for? Are we aware that it was for our salvation? If so, do we see more than the visitors did who photographed the big cross at St. Andrews Methodist Church? Do we merely stand and gape at it then go our way unmoved? May God have mercy upon us if we fail to accept the life Jesus intended us to have after suffering the pains of that cruel death just for us!

PRAYER: Our Father, whatever good is in our life today came as the result of that "Old Rugged Cross." Thank you for sending your Son into the world to give His life that we might live. In Jesus' name. Amen.

THOUGHT: The way we look at the cross determines every hour that follows.

21. IVORY PALACES

"All thy garments smell of myrrh, and aloes, and cassia, out of the ivory palaces, whereby they have made thee glad." (PSALM 45:8)

The refrain of the gospel song, "Ivory Palaces," was written on a visiting card, the only writing material available, in a small village store in North Carolina. The author and composer was the twenty-four year old talented Henry Barraclough, pianist for the evangelist, J. Wilbur Chapman. Chapman met the pianist the year before in England while conducting a preaching mission there. The young man soon became a part of the evangelistic team which included Charles M. Alexander, song leader and soloist, Albert Brown.

In 1915, Dr. Chapman was the preacher at the Presbyterian grounds, Montreat, North Carolina. One of the messages he was asked to give was a favorite of his entitled, "Ivory Palaces." Young Barraclough had heard this message many times, but on this occasion he was unable to force from his mind the thoughts expressed by the speaker.

After the service, Mr. Alexander invited some friends to go with him to the Blue Ridge Y.M.C.A. hostel not far away. Among those included was Henry Barraclough, rather quiet, still thinking about the recent sermon. Shortly they stopped at a little village store and in order to preserve his thoughts, he took a visiting card, the only writing material he could find at the moment, and on the back jotted down the familiar refrain.

That night, in his hotel he wrote three stanzas and composed the music. The next morning Mrs. Alexander and soloist, Albert Brown, sang for the first time this new hymn. Dr. Chapman felt the hymn wasn't finished and asked that he write a fourth stanza on the Lord's coming again. This he did and the complete gospel song soon appeared in hymnals all over the world. These are the words of the familiar chorus.

Out of the ivory palaces,
Into a world of woe,
Only His great eternal love
Made my Savior go.

* * * * * * *

I have in my possession a letter written very carefully but indicating the unsteady hand of age. The writer belonged to the generation preceeding this, and the words should bring a blush of shame to our faces. It reads as follows:

Dear Pastor,

"If you are at a loss, as to whom to assign your *very hardest prospects* for personal evangelism and knowing my unfitness, you think that I am worthy to undertake such a task, I will gladly seek to win them in Jesus' name."

It was signed by the initials of the writer. Can you grasp the depth of that life? It was not one seeking to win the easiest prospect. There are many who won't even volunteer for that. This person wasn't even asking for the hard prospect, but the very hardest.

There were to be no ivory palaces on earth for that sincere anonymous writer. Neither were there for Jesus. Instead He chose a cruel cross and gave His life for our salvation.

PRAYER: Dear Jesus, we do not always give thanks for what you have done for us, but we do today. We thank you for giving your life that we might live. Amen.

THOUGHT: If we are looking for courage let us turn our eyes on Jesus.

22. ARE YE ABLE

"Jesus answered and said, ye know not what ye ask. Are ye able to drink of the cup that I shall drink of, and to be baptized with the baptism that I am baptized with? They said unto him, We are able. (MATT. 20:22)

One of my friends in early youth was Earl Marlatt (1892-197). His influence on my life during his theological years at Boston did much to center my thoughts on attending Boston University after my conversion. He gave me a little book to read which didn't stimulate me at the time, but I have learned to treasure it through the years because he was the giver. Later he became my professor as well as friend at the University. He designated me as his "fellow-poet" and like the rest of the students I affectionately called him "the Duke."

In 1926 Marlatt was asked to write a hymn for a consecration service for the University's School of Religious Education.

Remembering the impression professor Marcus D. Buell made on him a few years before during a lecture on the reply of Jesus to the request of the mother of James and John, he began his poem. Thoughts began to flow as he concentrated on the words, "are ye able."

Like most of the ministerial students, I was pastor of a church, and Marlatt had his hymn printed the right size to be inserted in the hymnals. All over New England we young student pastors took that hymn to our churches, and within weeks our congregations were singing a hymn the rest of the country had never heard.

The tune was composed two years earlier by Henry H. Mason, who likewise was a student at Boston University, School of Theology. Mason had played it so many times that his classmates were already familiar with the music. It was only awaiting the hymn poem needed to make it live. That was now supplied by Earl Marlatt. The tune was called "Beacon Hill," because the School of Theology was located there at the time.

"Are ye able," said the Master
  "To be crucified with me?"
"Yea," the sturdy dreamers answered,
  "To the death we follow thee."

* * * * * * *

G. E. Montagne has an essay telling of a boy in church hearing for the first time the story of Calvary, and being brought to tears. In his new found experience he looked at the other worshippers around him and discovered that they remained unmoved. He wondered why no one else in the whole church seemed to be stirred. They listened as he did, but they acted as though they were listening to a broken record that merely goes round and round.

Do we not often act in the same manner when Jesus is trying to get our attention through His word? We are listening but we remain unmoved as though we were listening to a broken record.

These disciples didn't understand at the time, but they soon learned. When they cast aside their desire for power and faced a pagan world with the Gospel message, they knew for the first time what it meant to say, "Lord, we are able." No longer were they broken records but flaming evangels ready to suffer and die as He did. It might take that kind of persecution to make us understand also.

PRAYER: Lord, we say we are able while in our places of ease and plenty. Yet we know deep down in our hearts that what we need is courage to stand up for you when men revile you and tyrants persecute your followers. We pray for the kind of courage we should have to speak on your behalf when it is not easy to do so. Amen.

THOUGHT: Jesus conquered all before Him and that which empowered Him He offers us.

23. JESUS PAID IT ALL

"It was the third hour, and they crucified him." (MARK 15:25)

The Civil War years in America were not easy for either the North or South. There was not only a tremendous loss of life but a loss of much that people long held dear. Items of material value disappeared and multitudes lived for years in poverty. Jesus, however, remained. One to whom He was very precious was Elvina M. Hall. She was a choir member of the Methodist Episcopal Church in Baltimore. It was early in the year 1865 and the war was still dragging on and the casualties ever mounting. Elvina was meditating upon her own physical and spiritual condition. Her faith wasn't as strong as it used to be and as she thought on the turmoil in her own life as well as that of her divided nation, the Lord seemed to speak to her. She needed to write down the thoughts that were filling her mind so that she would not forget them, but how could she do it? She had no writing material, the church service was already under way and she was in a conspicuous place in the choir.

Finally it came time for the pastoral prayer; eyes should not be on her then, and she could write down her words in safety. She opened her choir book, "The New Lute of Zion," turned to the fly leaf and while the pastor continued his lengthy prayer, she began to write. From her pen that day flowed the words that people would soon be singing the world over. Moody and Sanky used the hymn, "Jesus Paid It All" wherever they went. Even before their time, the Evangelical Churches, especially the Methodists, were singing it as a revival hymn. It was also a camp meeting favorite. Therefore, in the choir loft of a Baltimore Church during the dark days of the Civil War a gospel song was written that is still a favorite of many today.

Jesus paid it all, All to Him I owe;
Sin had left a crimson stain,
He washed it white as snow.

* * * * * * *

During one of our Lenten services a girl from the junior department was deeply stirred. Following the benediction, she took from her purse every coin she had, wrote a note saying, "This is for God," and going to the altar, knelt, then placed what she had in her hand upon it. To her the money was important but that which mattered most was that she had found Christ. "This is for God," not only referred to her gift, but to her life also.

Many of the worshippers leaving the church said, "That was a good service." For this girl, it was more than a satisfying hour of worship. It was a time when she saw Christ upon the cross, sought His forgiveness, and came away a changed individual. Like Elvina Hall, she found in Jesus her "all in all."

PRAYER: We are thankful for that moment, O God, when we came face to face with your Son. Not only were our hearts warmed but our lives have been different ever since. Thank you Jesus. Amen.

THOUGHT: Whenever victory seems impossible in our life it is time to try Jesus.

24. I GAVE MY LIFE FOR THEE

"For even the Son of Man came not to be ministered unto, but to minister, and to give his life a ransom for many." (MARK 10:45)

She climbed almost to the summit of Europe's highest mountain, Mont Blanc. When her guide urged her to continue to the top she replied that she had accomplished all she had intended and to go further to reach that coveted goal would be nothing but vanity. In one of her letters she said, "The snow slopes were most entertaining to cross, and I enjoyed the scramble exceedingly." On her way back, sliding down those dangerous heights without skis, she almost lost her life. However, her comment on these treacherous slides was, "they were simply delicious." Yet Frances Ridley Havergal (1836-1879) was never a physically strong woman.

Her first attempt at writing a hymn was a disappointment. She considered it such a poor effort it was nearly destroyed before anyone else saw it. After reading the finished poem several times, Mrs. Havergal decided it was not worth saving and tossed it carelessly into the fireplace. Before the flames reached it, she thought to herself, "I shouldn't have done that," so she rescued the piece of paper and put it in her purse.

The inspiration to write this poem came as she read the motto, "I did this for thee, what hath thou done for me," over the head of Christ in the renowned picture, "Ecco Homo." "If that motto could do this to me," she reasoned, "it could do the same for others." She was right. Sometime after the fireplace incident, while visiting one who needed her ministry, she took the verses from her purse and read them to the semi-invalid. The words were so warmly received that she decided the poem was worth publishing after all.

I gave my life for thee,
  My precious blood I shed,
That thou might'st ransomed be
  And quickened from the dead.
I gave my life for thee.
  What hast thou given for me?

* * * * * * *

A college student who was uninterested in art was once persuaded by his mother to visit an art gallery to view the painting, "The Man of Galilee." After studying it from every angle, an attendant who had observed his interest said to him, "Great picture, isn't it?" "Yes," replied the student, "it is a great picture, and well named." Then the youth again softly stepped up to the painting and said, "O Man of Galilee, if I can in any way help you to do your work in the world, you can count on me."

Can the Master count on us to do what needs to be done in this hour? How much better off is He because of us? How much has His Kingdom advanced because He has chosen us to carry on His work? How many people have become better Christians because He has set us apart as His witnesses? What a tragedy it is to be chosen—yet fail! May the day quickly come when church members will say to the Lord, "What great thing can we do for you today?"

May we reverently kneel before Him, and say with the young

student, "O Man of Galilee, if I can in any way help you in my church, my community or in the world, you can count on me."

PRAYER: Because of your gift to us, Our Saviour, we have discovered the most rewarding life our Father could ever devise. Without hesitation, Jesus, may we give you all you require. Amen.

THOUGHT: The Master has infinitely more to offer us than we have to give Him.

25. CHRIST THE LORD IS RISEN TODAY

"He is not here; for he is risen as he said. Come, see the place where the Lord lay." (MATTHEW 28:6)

He was offered an estate by a wealthy land owner in Ireland. He refused, desiring to live on the small and unpredictable income that was his. If he had accepted the offer he might have become one of his country's outstanding citizens.

Poverty and sickness followed him all his life yet he refused to allow it to conquer him. There was nothing mediocre about him, for he was considered one of the best scholars and preachers of his generation. He traveled throughout the British Isles preaching wherever a crowd could be gathered. Every thought that came to his mind he turned into a hymn. He never went anywhere without writing material upon which he could record the words of each hymn as they came to him. One day he would be found preaching to the felons of Newgate and from there returning home to write hymns for them to sing. The next day he might be facing an army of rioters bent on killing him, yet in spite of this danger he continued to preach, calling on these would-be assassins to repent.

It was one of his early periods of sickness and his Moravian friend took him into his home so he could get the attention he needed. Scripture was read and prayer was made for his recovery. Then one night he heard a voice telling him to believe in the name of Jesus and he would be saved. He was so startled that he called his host and explained what had happened. His friend knew what had taken place and with shouts of praises he read Scripture concerning that experience and for the first time Charles Wesley (1707-1788) felt his sins forgiven. "I found myself at peace with God," he said, and that peace was to continue with him throughout the rest of his life. In 1739, thinking back over that wonderful experience and the great joy it brought to him together with the approaching Easter season, the words of a hymn came to his mind. As fast as he could write he put upon paper the words of "Christ the Lord is Risen Today."

The tune is of obscure origin and the Alleluia was added later.

Christ the Lord is risen today, Alleluia!
Sons of men and angels say, Alleluia!
Raise your joys and triumphs high, Alleluia!
Sing, ye heavens, and earth reply, Alleluia!

* * * * * * *

It was morning; morning at Joseph's tomb; morning in spite of the seal that had been placed upon the door and the rock that had been laid against it. The light of the sun had not quite penetrated the tomb, but the light of Eternity had; and it was morning within. Christ had risen and the whole world was bathed in a new light.

It was morning. Ah, yes, but far more important it still is. The most glorious news ever given is contained in the words, "He is not here. He is risen." No voice today can give a more assuring message than that and it came not from man but from God.

It is morning! Whatever else you accept, accept this. Let the glorious bells of Easter peal forth these words. Let the fragrance of the lilies waft it to your heart. Let the Easter music penetrate until it thrills your soul. It is morning, morning forever. The darkness of doubt and death have been dispelled. It is the eternal morning of the resurrection! Alleluia!

PRAYER: Our Heavenly Father, we thank you for the empty tomb with its message of life everlasting. May the assurance of an eternal morning grow stronger with each passing day. In the name of the risen Christ. Amen.

THOUGHT: The one hope for the world is that it be inoculated again with the life giving message of Easter.

26. I KNOW THAT MY REDEEMER LIVES

"He is not here: for he is risen, as he said. Come, see the place where the Lord lay." (MATTHEW 28:6)

He was raised in one of the finest Christian homes of his day. Love was showered upon him and his studies at school were supplemented by sound Christian education at home. At eighteen, like so many of his generation, he entered the Royal Navy. He had earlier been apprenticed to an oil dealer, but he considered the job dull and not the kind of work he wanted to do the rest of his life. The navy offered a far more exciting life, so he enlisted. He learned fast, but his education soon included more than what the navy taught. He selected as his companions those who lived a carefree, reckless life. He soon began to talk like them, carouse as they did and accepted their sinful habits. The pet lamb of a Christian household had become a black sheep.

His wildness was soon to end, however. He was severely wounded in a sea fight off Cape Lagos. Between pain and the fear of amputation he thought back over those early Christian years and he began to pray. Most of that night he prayed and God heard him and began a healing process that made it unnecessary to undergo the operation. When the surprised doctor looked at his wound the next morning he was aware that some kind of a miracle had taken place. Though no real conversion took place at that time he did make a vow that he would live again the life that was once his. After his discharge he went to live with his grandfather in London. He was a godly man and spent much time in prayer with his once wild grandson, Samuel Medley (1738-1799). Prayer was not the only thing offered. Scripture was regularly read and he listened to sermons from noted preachers. It was during the reading of one of Isaac Watts' sermons that he was converted. After recuperating he taught school for some years, and then began preparing for the ministry. For twenty-seven years he was a Baptist preacher in Liverpool where during that time he wrote many hymns, among them one of our best loved Easter hymns.

I know that my Redeemer lives;
What joy the blest assurance gives!
He lives, he lives who once was dead;
He lives, my everlasting Head!

* * * * * * *

During the depression of the 1930's, Bradley Memorial, a black church on Martha's Vineyard, had difficulty meeting its financial obligations. One Easter the church had no money at all for decorations. Someone gathered together enough change to buy one Easter lily. When the flower arrived the pastor thought of an aged and sick member who faced a bleak and lonely Easter Sunday. "Let's take the lily to her and brighten her Easter," he said. They all agreed and the lily was delivered early that morning. The following day a layman telling the story said, "We decorated our church that Sunday with paper flowers." Paper flowers at Easter! Why? Because a group of dedicated people caught the sacrificial spirit of Jesus and were willing to go without that someone else might be blessed. When mankind is assured that our Redeemer lives, greater sacrifices than this will take place.

PRAYER: Thank You Heavenly Father, for Easter. Because of your Son's resurrection, every day is a time of new life for us. In Jesus' name. Amen.

THOUGHT: With Christ in our heart every day is Easter.

27. IN THE GARDEN

"Mary stood without at the sepulchre weeping; and as she wept she stooped down, and looked into the sepulchre." (JOHN 20:11)

His mind was on the Lord as he sat near his organ in March, 1912. Stooping, he picked up his Bible and read once again the 20th chapter of John. This chapter was his favorite and he read it often. This time, however he suddenly became a part of this historic event.

"I seemed to be standing," he said, "at the entrance to a garden, looking down a gently winding path shaded by olive branches. A woman in white walked slowly into the shadows. It was Mary. As she came to the tomb, she bent over to look in, and leaning her head upon her arm, she wept. Turning, she saw Jesus standing beside her. So did I. Under the inspiration of this vision, I wrote as quickly as the words could be formed, the poem. That same evening I wrote the music."

This is how C. Austin Miles (1868-1946) came to write, "In the

Garden." He penned many of the hymns we sing, but this is without question, the favorite of many Christians.

I come to the garden alone,
  While the dew is still on the roses,
And the voice I hear, Falling on my ear,
  The Son of God discloses.

* * * * * * *

We are living in a garden also – the garden of this world, and we, too, often have tears in our eyes. For with our joys we face disappointments and sometimes overwhelming problems. We think we are fighting these difficult situations alone, but we are mistaken, for in that garden is Jesus and He comforts us as He seeks to lift our burdens. Are we aware of that fact? We should be, for Jesus is walking our streets just as He did the highways of Galilee. He is among those who worship in our churches, those who meditate and pray in their homes or who are facing some serious illness. Jesus can extend His hand and touch us and our fears, despondency and sorrow will disappear.

May we never forget the hour the risen Christ walked by our side. It may have been when we journeyed some lonely highway. In spite of our gloom new hope came to us as He reminded us that He will never leave or forsake us, and therefore we can never walk alone. Have we not heard His voice as He came to us in our sorrow saying, "Let not your heart be troubled, neither let it be afraid." He assured us that our loved ones were safe in the Father's house as He had promised. He always stands before our beds of pain with His healing touch telling us to arise and walk. It is that same love that causes Him to lift us when we have fallen and forgives us when we have sinned. Jesus is real and today, wherever you are He stands before you saying, "My peace I give unto you."

PRAYER: Our Father, in the midst of life's difficult situations, may we be aware of the presence of Your Son. Amen.

THOUGHT: Jesus never left the garden in which we walk daily. When we seek Him as Mary did we will find Him, and our bitter tears will become tears of joy.

28. BREAK THOU THE BREAD OF LIFE

"Thy word is a lamp unto my feet, and a light unto my path." (Psalm 119:105)

Mary A. Lathbury (1841-1913) was a Methodist minister's daughter and very talented. She had two brothers who were also ministers, the result of a Godly home. Mary was a writer of both poetry and prose and her works were widely published during her lifetime. She was also an artist and taught classes in art. More important, however, she was a dedicated church worker.

Her lasting contributions came through the new, fast growing Chautauqua movement. The assembly grounds surrounded Chautauqua Lake, New York state. Rev. John H. Vincent, who later became a Methodist Bishop developed the former camp meeting site into a ten week assembly for the study of the Bible and Sunday School methods. Dr. Vincent used whatever Bible hymns were available, but he was not satisfied because none seemed to have the message he needed.

He immediately thought of Miss Lathbury. She had worked with him when he was secretary of the Methodist Sunday School Union, and he was aware of her ability as a poet. He asked her therefore, if she would write such a hymn for the Chautauqua study classes. Promising that she would do her best she began work on her new assignment. She based her poem on the feeding of the multitude by Jesus. She realized that He, the Bread of Life, was feeding his followers on the Bread through His words. This was only one of two hymns that came from her pen at Chautauqua that year. The other is the well known evening hymn, "Day Is Dying in the West." William Sherwin was the director of music at the conference and composed the music for both hymns.

Break thou the bread of life,
  Dear Lord to me,
As thou did'st break the loaves
  Beside the sea;
Beyond the sacred page
  I seek Thee, Lord;
My spirit pants for thee,
  O living Word.

* * * * * * *

I sat by the bedside of a man who was desperately ill. I read selected passages of Scripture to him, but he turned a bewildered face in my direction and said, "It is no use, preacher, I guess those words were not meant for me." The words of the Bible were as a foreign language to him, for he had lived all of his life without that Book.

There always comes a time when Divine counsel will mean more than human counsel. Will we know where to find it when that time comes? The righteous must suffer with the unrighteous. At such a time the unprepared man rails against God accusing Him of being unfair. We who make the Bible our book can understand the meaning of suffering and know that it must come to the Christian as well as to those who become angry with God. His word will always be a lamp unto our feet and a light unto our path, but if we do not read that word we are unaware of the light it gives.

PRAYER: I am hungry for spiritual food, Lord. Break Thou the bread of life to me today. In Jesus' name. Amen.

THOUGHT: The word of God is the bread of life to our soul, and we need it as often as we need bread for our body.

29. THE CHURCH'S ONE FOUNDATION

"Christ also loved the church and gave himself for it." (EPH. 5:25)

He was one of the best athletes of his day, and like many other athletes he dedicated his life to Christ and became a successful clergyman. Although raised an Evangelical, he later became an Anglican while attending Pembroke College, Oxford. When a young man received this call from God he usually gave up his fighting spirit and became an apostle of peace. This was not entirely true of Samuel J. Stone (1839-1900).

In his younger days he wanted to be a soldier and his great physical strength would have caused him to go far in that branch of service. The call of God, however, became greater and he dedicated his life to the ministry. He seemed to be involved in controversy almost from the beginning. His first appointment in the Church of England was to a little Mission Chapel in a tough neighborhood. He was twenty-three at the time and still possessed his great strength. One day he saw a rough character mistreating a frightened little girl. He didn't simply watch but became involved, and immediately lunged at the bully, giving the offender a beating he would never forget.

He clashed with the civil authorities over the matter of public and parochial schools. He was in the midst of another controversy when a Bishop of the church in South Africa wanted to drop the first five books of the Old Testament from the Bible. It was then he wrote, "The Church's One Foundation." He was only twenty-seven years old at the time.

The Church's one foundation
Is Jesus Christ her Lord;
She is his new creation
By water and the word.

From heaven he came and sought her
To be his holy bride;
With his own blood he bought her,
And for her life he died.

* * * * * * *

I want the Church left in my life. I want it to be a part of all I do. I loved it when I gave up a promising career to enter the ministry and that love has never waned. That is why I understand the Church. I know its weakness and its strength. I know where it fails and why it fails. I likewise know the fascinating story of its tremendous success. No army has ever produced greater heroes than the Church and these heroic men and women have not all lived in past generations.

I not only know the Church, but I have seen it at work by the bed of pain and sickness. I have seen it ministering in the home of sorrow. I have looked upon it with joy as it brought hope to those who considered the future hopeless. I have heard the sobs of inner pain from those who have come to church with their sins and shortcomings. I have seen the light on the faces of multitudes who have found a solution to their baffling problems. I have seen the Church in action in every area of life because I have been there.

PRAYER: I love thy kingdom, Lord,
The house of thine abode,
The Church our blest Redeemer saved
With his own precious blood. Amen.

THOUGHT: We can like a church by merely attending, but we will not love the Church until we begin to do something for it.

30. THOU, WHOSE UNMEASURED TEMPLE STANDS

"Thou hast been a shelter for me, and a strong tower from the enemy. I will abide in thy tabernacle forever." (PSALM 61:3-4)

He was an old man, lonely and sad. His wife, of forty-five happy years, had died ten years before, and he was now standing before the house in which they were married. This was his first visit and tears filled his eyes as he walked through the familiar fields that surrounded the premises. With sobs he could not control he said, "There is not a spear of grass her foot has not touched."

He studied to be a lawyer, but after spending eight months in a town seven miles from his home, he returned with joy to his beloved woods and mountains. When someone asked him whether or not he liked the law profession he responded, "Alas!, Sir, the Muse was my first love."

He went regularly to worship, owning half a pew in the Congregational church. He would not stand for any vulgar action, or word and severely rebuked the offender. During all this time he yearned for his books, an opportunity to write poetry and to walk amidst the comforting shadows of the forest.

Now with his heart still filled with sorrow, viewing the surroundings that brought him the greatest joy, William Cullen Bryant (1794-1878) said, "I never wrote a poem that I did not repeat it to her and take her judgement on it." It was this gentle, courageous, dignified and spiritual man who wrote the hymn for this meditation. The first and third stanzas of this hymn concerning the church follow.

Thou, whose unmeasured temple stands,
  Built over earth and sea,
Accept the walls that human hands
  Have raised, O God to thee!

May erring minds that worship here
  Be taught the better way;
And they who mourn, and they who fear,
  Be strengthened as they pray.

It is sung to the familiar tune "Dundee" taken from the Scotch psalter.

* * * * * * *

Think of the memories that cluster around the church. On the pulpit is a Bible, usually given in memory of a loved one. The presence of the Bible indicates that God is speaking to His people. The lighted candles remind us that Christ lives and is still the world's light. Think of the memories that abound when one approaches the table for Holy Communion, with its inscribed words, "This do in remembrance of me!" The cross is there with its message of salvation. This and more stir vital memories. They make us realize why those who worshipped before us ended their earthly life in an era of peace and assurance. William Cullen Bryant had this and more in mind when he wrote the words to this touching hymn used for church dedications.

PRAYER: Speak, Lord, for your servant heareth. In Jesus' name. Amen.

THOUGHT: How big is our church according to God's measurement?

31. I LOVE THY KINGDOM, LORD

"Thy way, O God, is in the sanctuary." (PSALM 77:13)

Many of the great scholars of the church were also writers of well known hymns. Timothy Dwight (1752-1817) was one of these. He was born in Northampton, Mass., and was an unusual student, graduating from Yale with highest honors. He liked poetry and wrote many lengthy religious poems at an early age. At forty-three he was elected president of Yale College but his lasting fame came because of the hymns he wrote.

There was a great desire in his day to popularize the psalms of Isaac Watts. Therefore in 1800 the General Association of Connecticut asked if he would revise these psalms. He not only did what was requested but added many of his own translations. This hymn, "I Love Thy Kingdom, Lord," was one of these based on the one hundred and twenty-second psalm. He not only kept the spirit of this psalm, but produced a hymn that future generations could sing. Dr. Dwight was a very devout man and often when the college choir was singing he would join them, usually leading in ardent devotion. The tune is "St. Thomas," taken from Aaron Williams Psalmody.

I love Thy kingdom, Lord,
The house of Thine abode,
The church our blest Redeemer saved
With His own precious blood.

* * * * * * *

Some years ago there lived in my parish a couple who had separated. A divorce seemed imminent. One day a wedding was held in the church, and they attended, sitting as far apart as the church would permit. Before the prayer it was suggested that if any had broken the vows previously taken at the altar, this was the opportunity for rededication. Following the prayer and benediction an usher sought me asking if I was aware of any unusual commotion during the prayer. He then told how the man had left his seat and made his way to the other side of the church, where sitting by his wife, and taking her hand in his, they bowed in prayer. Shortly they left, arm in arm, tears of joy still in evidence. They had settled their difficulty in the sanctuary.

PRAYER: Oh, God, we thank You for your church. It is still the one hope for the world. We pray that the day will soon come when the problems that beset mankind will be settled through its influence. In the Master's name. Amen.

THOUGHT: Our most difficult problems may never be settled until we meet God in the sanctuary.

32. THE CHURCH IN THE WILDWOOD

"Take heed therefore unto yourselves, and to all the flock, over which the Holy Ghost hath made you overseers, to feed the church of God, which he hath purchased with his own blood." (ACTS 20:28)

The twenty-seven year old medical student was in a happy frame of mind. He had traveled nearly a hundred miles from Rush Medical School to Bradford, Iowa. He was on his way to Fredericksburg, but this was a stopping place for his stagecoach. While there he talked with the pastor of the Congregational Church and discovered they had no church building and had been meeting in various places since 1855. They desperately wanted a sanctuary but were unable to raise the money for such an undertaking. The student, while unable to help them financially, could help them decide on the best location for their church. He had already stood on the heights overlooking the village and upon viewing the valley below said to himself, "That's the spot." Talking to some friends later, the medical student, William S. Pitts, pointed out the location he had in mind saying, "I would build there and call it The Church in the Vale." He also suggested that he would paint it brown.

Upon returning to school he was unable to get the thought of the little brown church out of his mind. Finally the inspiration came, and he wrote both words and music to what eventually became one of our most beloved Gospel songs.

Some years later another minister was appointed to the little church at Bradford. He was told of the young man's vision and he urged his congregation to make that dream a reality. He also knew that everyone would have to work if a sanctuary was ever to be built. They had barely enough funds to buy the material. The project was heartily approved and while our Civil War was in progress these faithful members worked long hours each day until the structure was finished. Christmas, 1864, was a memorable occasion. The members and friends could now worship the Lord and sing their Christmas carols with a joy never before felt. The little brown church in the vale had become a reality.

Jesus loved the church and gave Himself for it. How far does our love go?

How sweet on a clear Sabbath Morning,
  To list to the clear ringing bell;
Its tones so sweetly are calling,
  Oh, come to the church in the vale.

* * * * * * *

A missionary tells of one of his members who had been arrested for a minor offense and was fined by the court. The next Sunday, as the service began, this man was not in his accustomed place, which was no surprise to the missionary. However, before the service was over the church door opened and the offender with head bowed in shame, entered and slowly walked to his usual seat. After the service the missionary warmly shook his hand and said that he really didn't expect him after what happened during the week. The reply this man made, who perhaps had not long been a convert, is unforgettable. Still with head bowed he said, "Where can a man go when he has done wrong, if he can't go to church?"

This is a note often missing in our world today. Many who consider themselves Christians rarely think of the church when they have done wrong. Yet we need our church as desperately as we need our home, especially when we have done something for which we are later ashamed.

Does our church mean that much to us? If not, maybe it is because we haven't put our time, material and talents into making our church a strong spiritual force in our community. The church bells should be to us the sweetest sound of the week.

PRAYER: Our Father, help us to love the church as Jesus loved it. He was willing to give His life for it. Make us to understand that this must be our desire also. In Jesus' name. Amen.

THOUGHT: Are we thrilled when we hear the Sabbath bells calling us to worship?

33. ONWARD, CHRISTIAN SOLDIERS

"And the Lord added to the Church daily such as should be saved." (ACTS 2:47)

In 1865, a year after his ordination, Sabine Baring-Gould (1834-1924) wrote the Hymn "Onward, Christian Soldiers." There is a story to the effect that when his Bishop heard the hymn he objected to the line, "With the cross of Jesus going on before," because it seemed too high church. Baring-Gould replied by changing the line to read, "With the cross of Jesus left behind the door." The bishop raised his hands in surrender when he heard these words, and agreed to the original line.

Baring-Gould wrote several hymns, but his most popular is the above which has consistently been used both as a challenging hymn and as a stirring composition for a marching band.

The hymn was written for a special occasion, when the children of his parish were to march on Whit Monday to a nearby village for the holiday festivities to be held there. Baring-Gould rearranged one of Haydn's symphonies for his new words, and on their way went the children, singing lustily. However, that tune failed to capture the imagination. It was not until six years later that these words came to the attention of one of England's leading composers, Sir Arthur S. Sullivan, whose compositions included symphonies, overtures, operettas as well as several hymn tunes. He decided to set it to music that would more aptly fit Baring-Gould's words, and in so doing caused a hymn that could have been forgotten to become one of the most exciting hymns of the church.

Onward, Christian Soldiers! Marching as to war
With the cross of Jesus going on before.
Christ, the royal Master, leads against the foe,
Forward into battle, see his banners go!

* * * * * * *

Think of the times we have sung "Like a mighty army moves the Church of God." But is she moving like a mighty army? Is she advancing toward the strongholds of evil in such force that those engaged in wrong, fear and tremble? Before we answer that question let us remind ourselves that we are the Church. Do we feel any responsibility in this area? Are we marching as a conqueror for the Lord? What about our triumphant sounds of victory? Are such victorious notes in evidence or have they ceased? In a sentence, are we only singing marching songs or are we really moving as a mighty army?

Have we not also, at some time or another, placed the cross behind the door? Jesus said, "Take up the cross daily and follow me." Do we? There is one thing of which we can be sure, when we place the cross behind the door we will also place love there, and faith and appreciation for His Church.

God's grace and mercy are present wherever you are. A miracle can happen in the church in which you worship if you would only take up again the cross and begin to carry it daily for the Master's sake.

PRAYER: Our Father, we do want to move as part of an army marching unto victory. May we take up our cross and follow Jesus as He commanded. Amen.

THOUGHT: No one who walks with Jesus is ever out of step.

34. BLEST BE THE TIE THAT BINDS

"This is my commandment, that ye love one another, as I have loved you." (JOHN 15:12)

He had a rough beginning and the years in between were not easy, but he ended life victoriously. His difficulties began at the age of twelve when he was left an orphan. The next year he was "bound out" as an apprentice to a tailor in Bradford, England. He was only 13 but his work began at 6 A. M. every morning and continued until eight o'clock at night. He was anxious for something better but he was unable to read and knew that when he was again free he would not be equipped for the work he desired. Therefore after work he secured some books and began to read by candlelight making sure that his master was unaware of what he was doing. It was while reading "Pilgrim's Progress" that he dedicated his life to Christ. At 15 he had a chance to listen to George Whitefield and after the sermon confided to him that he wanted to be a preacher.

He never lost that desire and not many years later he began to preach in and around Bradford. Eventually he came to the attention of a small Baptist Church in the nearby village of Wainsgate. The houses were scattered, many of the people were illiterate, vice flourished and profanity was heard everywhere. It was not an easy church to serve and his salary of $100 a year didn't make it any easier. In spite of the seemingly unfruitful field, the church continued to grow under his leadership. So did his family, four children in five years. He told his officials he couldn't remain at that salary, so they promised him an increase of 25 pounds if he would take it in produce rather than money. It wasn't long before he realized that his financial situation was getting worse instead of better.

Then a break came. Dr. Gill, pastor of Carter's Lane Baptist Church in London was forced to retire because of ill health. An invitation arrived at Wainsgate asking if Rev. John Fawcett (1740-1817) would come and preach in their church so that the congregation could hear him. He accepted the invitation and was so well received that before he left he was asked to come and be their preacher. John hurried home with the good news and they soon began to pack. No more living on wool and potatoes for them.

The day for moving arrived. His parishioners, with tears in their eyes, helped him get ready. There was no levity on the part of the sorrowful, silent people who carefully carried household articles to the wagon. His wife was so affected, she said to her husband, "I feel we are making a mistake to leave." His answer was that he felt the same. They knew then that it was impossible for them to go, so the wagon was unpacked and they decided to spend the rest of their lives with these people who loved them so much. Later Fawcett wrote the words of a hymn that will be sung as long as hymn books are printed, "Blest be the Tie that Binds." That tie bound them together until the hymn writer's death forty five years later!

Blest be the tie that binds
Our hearts in Christian love;
The fellowship of kindred minds
Is like to that above.

* * * * * * *

Rev. Bob Carlson and his wife served a Methodist Church on the Florida Keys. During that pastorate a destructive hurricane swept the Keys and Bob and his wife lost their lives. When the storm abated some of his brother ministers moved into the area to search for their bodies, but without success. They returned to Miami hoping to find someone who had seen the Carlsons during the storm. Inquiring among the hospitalized refugees, they met one who remembered seeing the preacher and his wife in overalls, helping neighbors board up their windows. He continued, "I imagine the Reverend and his wife drowned. If you find them they will have on overalls and I expect there will be some rusty nails in his pocket."

Days later they found Bob and his wife submerged under the swollen waters, held down by seaweed. One of the preachers remarked, "They have on overalls." Then he reached in Bob's pocket and drew out a handful of rusty nails.

Many may be indifferent to the plight of their fellow men, but not the Christian. Somewhere upon him will be found the "rusty nails" of loving service.

PRAYER: "Bind us together, Lord, bind us together
With cords that cannot be broken.
Bind us together, Lord, bind us together, Lord,
Bind us together in love." Amen.

THOUGHT: The test of real love, is not just in how much we are willing to do for ourselves or those dear to us, but in how much we are willing to do for others.

35. TELL ME THE OLD, OLD STORY

"My mouth shall speak the praise of the Lord: and let all flesh bless his holy name forever and ever." (PSALM 145:21)

In the summer of 1867, Major-General Russell of the British Army was addressing the delegates of an international Y.M.C.A. convention in Montreal, Canada. He reminded them that he was not about to make a speech, but to read a poem that had stirred him deeply. Tears filled his eyes before he had finished, and the audience was deeply moved. The poem Russell read was written by A. Katherine Hankey (1834-1911), an English banker's daughter, while she was convalescing from a serious illness. She spent her idle moments writing a poem of fifty verses, from which came two of our hymns of inspiration.

She was only thirty years old at the time, but the doctor warned her that her life was in danger unless she spent a long time in bed. It was difficult for her to give up her Bible teaching and missionary work, but she wisely accepted his advice. Making sure she had plenty of reading and writing material at hand she prepared to spend the year suggested by the doctor in bed. It was during this period that she wrote her long poem.

Tell me the old, old story,
  Of unseen things above.
Of Jesus and His glory,
  Of Jesus and His love.
Tell me the story simply,
  As to a little child,
For I am weak and weary,
  And helpless and defiled.

* * * * * * *

At one of our Official Board retreats, a young Jewish convert was invited to give his testimony. He had conducted business in the city for many years and a large number of our church people knew him. When he spoke, he told how members of a very small denomination continually talked to him about Jesus as he waited on them. Although irritated at first, these conversations eventually led to his conversion. "I would never have been a Christian," he said, "if it had not been for these devout people," and then named many of them. One of our outstanding women officials, a very dedicated and sincere person, was to speak next. "This gentleman knew me," she said, "but he didn't know my name although I have been in his store many times." Then she hesitated and added in all humility, "But you see, I didn't talk to him about Jesus."

Are we talking about Jesus? Are we telling the old, old story? As Christians we are commissioned to tell the story of Jesus. May we not fail Him for he has faith in us.

PRAYER: Our Father, forgive us when we talk about so many things, but fail to find time or opportunity to speak the necessary word on behalf of your Son. We have been blessed far beyond anything we deserve. Teach us that our blessings would be multiplied if we were more eager to express our faith to others.

In the Master's name. Amen.

THOUGHT: The growth of Christianity is a tribute to those who possessed an overwhelming desire to speak for Jesus.

36. JUST AS I AM

"Him that cometh unto me I will in no wise cast out." (JOHN 6:37)

Charlotte Elliott (1789-1871) who was called a "sunbeam," was not always looked upon as such. In fact, there was a time when she was irritable and bitter. It was an outstanding clergyman who helped her see the error of her ways. As a talented young woman she was being praised for her accomplishments. This she enjoyed and her face was wreathed in smiles. Rev. Caesar Malan, however, felt that there was something missing in her life. To him she seemed vain and worldly rather than humble and thankful for the gifts God had bestowed upon her. In spite of her failing health she gave little thought of her spiritual condition.

The noted Swiss minister and musician was an invited guest at her home. During the dinner hour the conversation included the question of whether or not Charlotte was saved. Immediately she became angry and hinted that her guest should mind his own business. After the dinner she and Dr. Malan had a heated discussion concerning her physical and spiritual condition. Charlotte's anger eventually evaporated and she realized how badly she had treated a friend who was only trying to help her. Apologizing for her rudeness she asked how she could become a Christian. "All you have to do," he answered, "is to go to Jesus just as you are."

The years passed and she became more and more of an invalid. Every year she received a letter of spiritual encouragement from Dr. Malan and it always reminded her of how mean and rude she was on that previous occasion. She was no longer bitter. In fact she was faithfully practicing the spiritual exercise he had suggested after their memorable encounter.

Fourteen years passed and instead of being an irritable invalid she had become so sweet and affectionate she was called a "sunbeam." She had matured spiritually also and Dr. Malan's words to come to Jesus just as you are were always on her mind. That year, when she was forty-seven years old, she decided to write as her spiritual autobiography the beautiful hymn we know. It is one of the most moving and soul-saving hymns of the church.

> Just as I am, without one plea,
> But that Thy blood was shed for me,
> And that Thou bidd'st me come to Thee,
> O Lamb of God I come! I come.

* * * * * * *

Are we willing to come to Jesus just as we are? To us our life might seem clean and decent, yet there are times when we are not satisfied with the way we live. We might not know what we lack but Jesus does and He asks us to come to Him just as we are. He has more to offer us than we ever thought possible. "Ask," He said, "and ye shall receive." Have we asked for help to correct the errors of our ways?

PRAYER: Lord Jesus, show me what there is in my life that is displeasing to You. What do I lack? What change would you have me make? I pray for the necessary help to correct my mistakes, that I may receive the power you promised me. Amen.

THOUGHT: Coming to Jesus not only involves accepting His invitation, but accepting Him.

37. ALMOST PERSUADED

"Almost thou persuadest me to be a Christian." (ACTS 26:28)

Many hymns have been written following a soul-stirring sermon that has made a lasting impression on some listener's heart. "Almost persuaded" is an example. Philip P. Bliss (1838-1876) while waiting for a train slipped into an Ohio church while the evening service was in progress. The preacher, Mr. Brundage, used as his closing words, "He who is almost persuaded is almost saved, but to be almost saved is to be entirely lost." He had been preaching on the familiar story of Paul before King Agrippa. Bliss was so impressed and stirred by these final words of the sermon that he jotted them down intending to use them later. Several days passed but these words were still upon his mind, and his heart told him that now was the time to write that hymn. The result was that he wrote both words and music to a gospel song that is still a blessing to many. It has been estimated that thousands have been led to Christ through the singing of this one sacred number alone.

"Almost persuaded" now to believe;
"Almost persuaded" Christ to receive;
Seems now some soul to say
"Go Spirit, go thy way,
Some more convenient day
On Thee I'll call."

* * * * * * *

February 9, 1896, the schooner, *Florida*, was out of control in a violent storm, drifting helplessly towards Salisbury Beach, Massachusetts. Not long afterwards she went to the bottom taking every member of the crew with her.

Three nights before, the Captain and crew were present at the Seaman's Bethel in Vineyard Haven. They were in a happy mood during the social hour as they mingled with crewmen from other vessels and ate their cake and ice cream. Chaplain Madison Edwards, however, was watching his barometer which was showing signs of a possible storm. These storms were a concern to him especially when the vessels were to leave early in the morning. He urged them to wait but the captain insisted that they could weather whatever storm might arise.

In a simple direct fashion, during the devotional service that followed, the chaplain pleaded with those present to yield their lives to Christ. Three members of the *Florida* did, but two of the crew brushed him aside with the words, "We'll accept Jesus when we get home." He knew this was only an excuse. He had heard it before, and with an inner pain he did not show he reminded them that this could be their last chance.

Laughing merrily, they returned to their boat. These were the two whose faces and words haunted the chaplain when the news of the wreck reached him. "God grant," he wrote, "that they found peace as they clung to the rigging that dreadful night, and reached the home where no storms ever came. I shall long remember the faces of those two boys as I talked to them about their soul's salvation."

PRAYER: Our Father, teach us our need of You. Show us how dangerous it is to live without the consciousness of Your presence. Subdue our hearts' rebellion and cause us to turn unto you that we may receive mercy and be abundantly pardoned. Amen.

THOUGHT: God is speaking this moment. Are you listening?

38. JESUS LOVER OF MY SOUL

"For thou hast been a strength to the poor, a strength to the needy in his distress, a refuge from the storm, a shadow from the heat, where the blast of the terrible ones is as a storm against the wall." (ISAIAH 25:4)

The hymn, "Jesus Lover of My Soul," is considered by many one of the best examples of faith and hope to be found in hymnology. It was written by Charles Wesley (1707-1788) not long after his own heartwarming experience. There have been many stories concerning the origin of this hymn, each apparently the product of someone's imagination. The most prevalent tells of his seeking a hiding place amidst the persecution that surrounded the early Methodist preachers. Jane Lawrie Moore claims to have hidden him under a hedge in her back garden when he was chased by an angry mob. This story might have died there, but her granddaughter, at the time living in America, told her pastor that this story given by her grandmother was true. The story was then repeated in sermons from many pulpits. However, the Methodists were not persecuted in 1740 when this hymn was written. That came later. The oft repeated tale of the dove flying to Wesley for shelter is exciting, but hardly fact.

Whatever was on the hymn writer's mind, there was one experience he never would forget. A few years earlier, on his return from America he survived a severe storm. Waves crashed over the boat and it was expected to sink at any moment. Frightened as he was, Charles Wesley sought to calm the passengers and upon stepping from the ship he immediately knelt down and thanked God for deliverance. This may not be the only reason for the hymn, but the words of the first stanza would indicate that he had not forgotten that perilous voyage.

Jesus, lover of my soul,
  Let me to thy bosom fly,
While the nearer waters roll,
  While the tempest still is high:
Hide me, O my Savior, hide,
  Till the storm of life is past;
Safe into the haven guide;
  O receive my soul at last!

* * * * * * *

We were driving through the White Mountains of New Hampshire, when the clouds were so low and thick, that even the peaks could not be seen. Then as we reached the brow of a hill, the overcast suddenly shifted long enough for us to see the top of Mount Washington. Although we were still surrounded by clouds, the sun was shining in all its beauty on the heights that towered above us.

So it is in life. Evil forces may move in our midst, hatred seem triumphant over Christian love, the power of brute force appear ready to destroy the peace of the world. These are ominous clouds indeed. Yet, there is abundant hope, for above these fearful clouds is the Eternal God and He has the last word.

PRAYER: When unwanted clouds surround our life, O God, may we know that You will support and sustain us until the darkness disappears. In Jesus' name. Amen.

THOUGHT: If we are fearful let us remember the light above the clouds, and take heart.

39. ROCK OF AGES

"And he said, the Lord is my rock, and my fortress, and my deliverer." (2 SAMUEL 22:2)

Rock of Ages was written in the midst of a bitter controversy. Augustus M. Toplady (1740-1778) an Anglican clergyman and the writer of the hymn, was a man of culture and ability. He was an advanced Calvinist and very sincere in his belief. He preached that only the elect could be saved. The man he fiercely denounced was John Wesley, who believed that salvation was available to all.

Toplady was a fiery antagonist, conscientious and a tireless worker. In his early thirties his health began to fail but that did not dampen his spirit. He accused Wesley of hiding behind his preachers, letting them do the talking. He wrote, "Let Mr. Wesley fight his own battles . . . let his cobblers keep to their stalls, his tinkers mend their brazen vessels, his barbers confine themselves to their blocks and basins, his blacksmiths blow more suitable coals than those of controversy." Wesley tried to avoid this type of destructive criticism but found it impossible to do so. Even as Toplady's health deteriorated he still continued to denounce Wesley's theology. He finally died of tuberculosis on August 11, 1778. He was thirty-eight years of age.

He had written the words to the hymn, "Rock of Ages" three years earlier while taking shelter in the cleft of a rock during a sudden storm. His mind was always active and as the words of his hymn began to form, he sought some material he could use to write on. He searched his pockets and all he could find was a playing card. Upon that worldly item his immortal hymn was written.

Rock of Ages, cleft for me,
Let me hide myself in Thee;
Let the water and the blood,
From thy wounded side which flowed,
Be of sin the double cure,
Save from wrath and make me pure.

* * * * * * *

I never look at a congregation without wondering what tragedies might be there, what agony of mind, what hardening of heart. How many sitting in some congregation every Sunday are unwanted, unloved or misunderstood? How many are lonely? How many wonder whether or not life is worth living? Oh, the secrets that are locked in every heart and the pain that arises from those secrets! You and I are always thrown back on Jesus. Without Him the storms of life will increase. They never diminish. He is our rock and shelter in the storms of life. He is our refuge and our strength. Only as we seek the shelter of that Rock will we find the peace and calm we need.

PRAYER: Jesus, You are our refuge and our strength, the unmovable rock to which we can go for shelter. Thank you for offering us a place of safety when the sudden squalls of life overtake us. Amen.

THOUGHT: The hour that called for a song from the lips of the Master came when He left behind the seclusion of the upper room for a cross.

40. AMAZING GRACE

"God, who is rich in mercy, for his great love wherewith he loved us even when we were dead in sins, hath quickened us together with Christ, by grace ye are saved." (EPH. 2:4-5)

When John Newton (1725-1807) was six years old, his mother died of tuberculosis. Before her death she spent hours with the child teaching him Bible stories, during which time she dedicated his life to Christ and the ministry. His father was a sea captain and after his son spent a few years at school he decided to make him a part of his crew. However, his youth ended amidst debauchery and failure. His father had enough and demanded that he leave the ship. No one wanted to hire a trouble-maker, so he spent much of his time drinking and carousing, eventually ending in jail. While there he considered suicide but was released before he could act upon his desire. His next move was to enter the slave trade. One night, with his ship's hold full of slaves, he encountered a terrifying storm. For him it was God's handwriting upon the wall. He remembered his mother's early religious training and decided that after delivering his cargo he would leave the sea. To do so didn't come that easy for it was six years later when he finally stepped ashore and became the tide surveyor of Liverpool.

At 39 he began to prepare himself for the ministry to which his mother had dedicated his life. Later he wrote "Amazing Grace." The tune is an early American melody and the last verse was added some years later during the early Camp Meeting days.

Amazing grace! how sweet the sound
That saved a wretch like me!
I once was lost, but now am found,
Was blind, but now I see.

* * * * * * *

How well we remember that hour when Jesus first touched us. What a thrill that experience gave us. How is it today? Is there still a quiver in our heart? Is there still a desire to serve the Lord? Like Newton we look upon that divine encounter as our spiritual birthday. Although we lacked the ability to write a hymn about that happy occasion we couldn't stop talking about it.

If that transforming experience was genuine it should be revealed in our lives more clearly in each passing year. God never expected that experience to abruptly end. Like all births a spiritual birth is only the beginning. Others notice when we grow physically. Is our spiritual growth as easily discernible?

PRAYER: Our Father, we have all been saved from something, but we know that we cannot stop there. Help us to develop and grow that others might see a bit of Jesus in us. Amen.

THOUGHT: What a consolation it is when we spiritually fail, to realize how precious we are in the sight of the Lord.

41. I LOVE TO TELL THE STORY

Howbeit Jesus suffered him not, but saith unto him, Go home to thy friends, and tell them how great things, the Lord hath done for thee, and hath had compassion on thee." (Luke 5:19)

In the mid 1860's Miss A. Katherine Hankey (1834-1911), daughter of an English banker, published a small volume called "Heart to Heart," in which was a lengthy poem of fifty verses. From the first section of this poem, entitled "The Story Wanted," came the words of the hymn "Tell Me the Stories of Jesus." From the second section, entitled "The Story Told" came the words of "I Love to Tell the Story." During a lengthy illness she is said to have spent ten months writing her poem which produced the words for two well known hymns.

Katherine Hankey spent much of her time organizing Bible classes for both rich and poor in England. This made it possible for her not only to minister to unfortunate women, but also to tell them the story of Jesus. This had long been her desire and when she was stricken with a serious illness and could no longer witness to others, at least for many months, she decided to put her thoughts on paper. During that long period of sickness her mind was centered upon Jesus and how she could tell the story of his love.

> I love to tell the story Of unseen things above,
> Of Jesus and His glory, Of Jesus and His love.
> I love to tell the story, Because I know 'tis true;
> It satisfies my longings As nothing else can do.

* * * * * * *

When Stanley went to Africa in search of Livingston, he was not a Christian. He didn't take that hazardous journey in order to become one. He was a daring newspaper reporter who was anxious to find Livingston, because in so doing he would find a good story. He found the missionary and with it a better story than he had anticipated. It was the story of his own conversion. How did it happen? It was not because Livingston preached to him. Here is what Stanley said, "When I saw his untiring efforts spending himself for Christ and human need, I became a Christian, though he never spoke a word to me about it." A good life has led many to Christ and it is always a happy day when that great event takes place.

We witness by our words but our greatest witness is by our life. We cannot pass on to others what we do not possess. We cannot lead another to faith in God if we do not have that faith. It is impossible to pass on goodness, even to our children, if we ourselves are not good. Certainly a Christ-like spirit cannot be imparted if we do not possess one. If we do not have Christ in our life we can pass on our vices as well as our virtues. If we are going to tell the story of Jesus we have to live that story, not once in a while, but daily.

PRAYER: Heavenly Father, may we never be ashamed to talk about you. May we know, however, that we cannot be a successful witness unless we practice what we preach. Give us wisdom and tact as we present Your Son to a world yearning for someone in whom they can put their trust. In Jesus' name. Amen.

THOUGHT: The Gospel was never meant to be a keepsake.

42. HE KEEPS ME SINGING

"Fear thou not; for I am with thee: be not dismayed; for I am thy God: I will strengthen thee; yea, I will help thee; yea, I will uphold thee with the right hand of my righteousness." (ISAIAH 41:10)

Some years ago the brother-in-law of Luther B. Bridges (1884-1948) and I held a series of revival services in a New York state church. During our week together he repeated the tragic story that produced the hymn "He Keeps Me Singing."

Luther Bridges was not only talented but a very dedicated Methodist preacher. In 1910 this twenty-six year old pastor was invited to hold revival services not far from his own parish. His wife and three young sons remained at home with relatives. The last night of his two-week services had come to a successful conclusion, but for some reason he had difficulty in getting to sleep. He had a vague feeling that something was wrong, but he had no idea what it could be. At two o'clock that morning there came a knock on his room door. A telephone call had been received conveying the shocking message that his entire family—his wife and young sons—had been consumed in a fire that destroyed the house in which they were staying. The broken hearted husband hurried home, and all that was found of his loved ones' remains could be fitted into one small box. Some time later he wrote the words and music to a song of victory and faith that has given hope and courage to multitudes of people.

There's within my heart a melody
Jesus whispers sweet and low,
Fear not, I am with thee, peace be still,
In all of life's ebb and flow.

Chorus

Jesus, Jesus, Jesus, sweetest name I know
Fills my every longing,
Keeps me singing as I go.

* * * * * * * *

Like Luther B. Bridges we need the companionship of Jesus. We do not know when we will be forced to face a heart breaking experience. It might be in our home tonight. It could be on the highway tomorrow. It might be somewhere in the dim distance, but whenever it comes we need to be on the right terms with God.

We do not choose the rough places of life. We do not deliberately run in the direction of tragedy. However, no one can go through life filled only with sunshine. Storms will also have to be faced and conquered. Therefore we dare not go it alone. We need Jesus for He is the only one who can sustain us when tragedy strikes. It is He who still comforts us in such an hour with the words, "I will not leave you comfortless."

PRAYER: Our Father, we know it is not easy to sing praises when loved ones leave us. Those of us who have gone through that experience also know that You have a way of slipping around us those everlasting arms of comforting love. May we ever be thankful for that. In Jesus' name. Amen.

THOUGHT: A fair weather faith is only a sunshine faith. What we need is a faith that can master the storms.

43. WONDERFUL WORDS OF LIFE

"Then said Jesus unto the twelve, will ye also go away? Then Simon Peter answered him, Lord, to whom shall we go? Thou hast the words of eternal life." (JOHN 6:67-68)

He was born with music in his soul, and during his short life became one of America's greatest hymn writers and composers. He was also born in poverty in a Pennsylvania log cabin. It is recorded that his parents named him Philipp, but later in life he changed it to Philip and allowed the extra p to be his middle initial.

He married in his early twenties and with a horse named Fanny and a portable organ, he spent the winters conducting music schools in towns and villages that provided him a place to meet with his young pupils. It was D. L. Moody who encouraged him to give up his teaching and become a song leader and soloist in evangelistic campaigns. Because of his rich baritone voice he soon became a much sought after soloist and song leader. He appeared with the major evangelists of his day, all the while writing both words and music to hymns that will live through the years.

Midway through the last century, Fleming H. Revell, of the Revell Publishing Company, decided to publish a religious periodical called "Words of Life." He asked this Spirit-filled sacred hymn writer if he would prepare an inspirational message for the occasion. He accepted his friend's request and immediately began to think of what he should write. The more he concentrated on the words of Jesus the more he realized how much those words had meant to mankind. With his Bible opened to John 6:67-68 he began to work and within a short time he had completed the words and music to "Wonderful Words of Life."

At the height of his career, while only 38 years old, Philip P. Bliss (1838-1876) and his wife, Lucy, perished in a flaming railroad wreck near Ashtabula, Ohio. With his untimely death there passed one of America's great writers and composers of Gospel songs.

Sing them over again to me,
  Wonderful words of life:
Let me more of their beauty see,
  Wonderful words of life.

* * * * * * *

Jesus continually stands before us always presenting his wonderful words of life. He has a message for each one. His message is not like that of the world. It is not like the words of non-Christian religions or the many cults that confront us. His thoughts are not intended to cover up, confuse or cause one to ignore eternal values. It is the simple, yet glorious message of salvation through Him. It reveals the hand that heals the blind eyes that men may see.

PRAYER: Dear Lord, when someone is seeking Jesus or when they want the words of life, may I be understanding and loving as I answer their request. In Jesus' name. Amen.

THOUGHT: Words are always important but the words of Jesus are packed with power.

44. O HAPPY DAY

"My spirit hath rejoiced in God my Saviour." (LUKE 1:47)

"My baby is dead," sobbed the distressed mother as she looked upon the inert form of her new born son. He certainly appeared dead and she had every reason to believe that he was. Of her nineteen children all but two died in infancy. However, she was mistaken on this occasion, for her twentieth child not only lived but became one of the best known hymn writers of his generation.

His mother was a very pious woman and taught the boy important verses from the Bible by way of Dutch tiles on their chimney. These instructions stopped all too soon, for while still a youth both of his parents died. Nevertheless, he continued his studies and later became an outstanding scholar. He was ordained in 1722 and became pastor of the Congregational Church in Northampton, England. He was also principal of the Theological school in that place. It was his habit to arise at five A. M. and most of his writings were done at that time. It was during these early hours that he prepared poems to be used at the conclusion of his sermons. Many of these became the familiar hymns of the church. The hymn for this meditation by Philip Doddridge (1702-1751) was written when the sun was bathing and cleansing the world with its light. For him, this is what Jesus did when He washed his sins away and made him clean.

When Philip's benefactor, Dr. S. Clark, died in December, 1750, Doddridge conducted his funeral service, but the journey was too much for the frail body that was already weakened by tuberculosis. Shortly thereafter he went to Lisbon hoping that the climate would help him regain his strength. However, he never returned to England but died a year later. He was a devout soul, loved by all who knew him, and during his long siege of ill health, his faith and trust in God never wavered.

It was when the sun was rising in all of its brilliance that this saintly man thought of the happiest day of his life and began to write:

O happy day, that fixed my choice
  On thee, my Saviour and my God!
Well may this glowing heart rejoice,
  And tell its raptures all abroad.

* * * * * * *

Someone has written a story about a conversation that took place between Jesus and Zacchaeus. Jesus said, "Zacchaeus, I expected you to give back the money you took unjustly from others, but why did you give back so much?" Zacchaeus answered, "Because, Master, when I looked in your eyes I saw the man God wanted me to be."

Let us look into the eyes of Jesus for only in this way will we see the kind of person God intends us to be. Philip Doddridge looked in the face of Jesus early in life, and became the kind of a man God wanted him to be.

PRAYER: Our Father, we can never fully thank you for sending your Son into the world to save us from our sins. It was a happy day when Jesus washed our sins away. Thank you, Heavenly Father, for that gift of your love. In Jesus' name. Amen.

THOUGHT: We will only become Christ-like when the spirit that was his becomes ours.

45. HE LEADETH ME

"He maketh me to lie down in green pastures; He leadeth me beside the still waters. He restoreth my soul; He leadeth me in paths of righteousness for his name's sake." (PSALM 23:2-3)

The son of the governor of New Hampshire was a scholar and competent writer. He was born in Boston and graduated from the Newton Theological Institution, where he later became a Hebrew instructor. In 1862, while still a young Baptist preacher, he was asked to preach at the First Baptist Church in Philadelphia. His message that evening was on the 23rd Psalm, particularly the leadership of God. At that very moment the north and south were engaged in a fierce struggle. Strong leadership was needed on both sides and this young preacher knew who that Leader had to be.

After the service, words concerning that leadership seemed uppermost on the mind of Joseph Henry Gilmore (1834-1918), and he could hardly wait until he had placed them on paper. This was the way he described the occasion: "The blessedness of God's leadership so grew upon me that I took out my pencil, wrote the hymn just as it stands today, handed it to my wife and thought no more about it.

She sent it, without my knowledge, to the *Watchman* and *Recorder.*"

Gilmore then goes on to say that three years later he went to preach in the Second Baptist Church in Rochester. While waiting in the chapel he wondered what hymns they were accustomed to singing. He picked up a hymnbook, opened it, and on that very page was the hymn, "He Leadeth Me." "That," he said, "was the first time I knew my hymn had found a place among the songs of the church."

> He leadeth me: O blessed thought!
> O words with heavenly comfort fraught!
> Whate'er I do, where e'er I be,
> Still 'tis God's hand that leadeth me.

* * * * * * *

The Saviour not only goes before me preparing a way through the problems, difficulties and dangers of life over which I can safely pass, but even after the road is prepared He is still my leader. His hand is always extended in my direction. The responsibility of accepting Him as my leader rests with me.

Often, for my own protection "He maketh me to lie down in green pastures." Only in this way can I achieve the poise and inner calm sufficient to overcome the pressure of this turbulent hour.

"He leadeth me," not occasionally, but constantly. Many times have I sought to lead Him. His way did not seem to be the most attractive for the modern day. Sometimes I have impatiently left Him behind. How slow He seemed to one accustomed to speed. But always when I returned He was still ready to lead. He did not become impatient with me.

"He leadeth me beside still waters." He ushers me in to quiet places, not given by the world, that I might have the opportunity to think and meditate. Church worship, communion, private devotions, the study of God's Word—these are the waters that refresh me.

PRAYER: Our Father, may our desire to follow your Son be so real that at His word we will immediately arise and do whatever He has for us to do. In Jesus' name. Amen.

THOUGHT: Only as we follow Jesus will we, in turn, be worth following.

46. THE SOLID ROCK

"And the Lord said, behold there is a place by me, and thou shalt stand upon a rock." (Exodus 33:21)

As a cabinet maker Edward Mote (1797-1874) was a success, but he was really not happy. He wanted to do more for the Lord than his limited time would permit. It wasn't always that way. He was raised by unbelieving parents who sent him to a school where a Bible was not allowed to be read. He was not happy there either, for his young heart yearned for something more than what he was receiving. Then one day he found what he was seeking. He was only sixteen when he listened to a sermon by John Hyatt at Tottenham Court Road Chapel and was greatly impressed. The weeks that followed were exciting ones. The unbelief that had troubled his mind for so long soon vanished. He had discovered One who made life worth living.

After finishing his education he was employed in a woodworking shop, eventually saving money enough to buy his own. Yet something was lacking. He spent many hours writing poetry and other articles, primarily on spiritual matters. One day, when he was thirty-four years old, as he was on his way to his cabinet shop, these words suddenly came to his mind. "On Christ the Solid Rock, I stand; All other ground is sinking sand." The more he thought about these words the greater became his desire to turn them into a poem. Shortly after arriving at his place of business, and while these words were still fresh upon his mind, he entered his office and began writing. In spite of the many interruptions, before the day ended he had written the four verses that are now familiar to all Christians. Edward Mote might not have been aware of it at the moment but in finishing the poem he had authored one of the great hymns of the church.

Although he liked his work, his mind was not completely at ease. He wanted to become a minister, and at the age of fifty-five he was ordained, eventually becoming pastor of the Baptist church in Horsham, Sussex. He was now happy and remained there until his death twenty-six years later. Thus the boy who started life as an unbeliever left to the world one of the great hymns of faith.

My hope is built on nothing less
Than Jesus' blood and righteousness;
I dare not trust the sweetest frame,
But wholly lean on Jesus' name.

On Christ, the solid rock, I stand
All other ground is sinking sand.

* * * * * * *

When I dedicated my life to the ministry, I did it by way of an altar call. It seemed impossible that my faith would ever wane. However, when I entered theological school, I discovered that much I believed was out of harmony with modern thought. I had to unlearn a good deal and the process was painful. Later I became pastor of a little church in a nearby state. For nearly a year the struggle continued. I was not happy. With doubts that almost overwhelmed me I sought to bring messages of faith to my people. Finally the victory was won, but only after wrestling long and earnestly in prayer. I am thankful now for that period, for it provided a faith nothing could destroy and prepared me for the many difficult and painful situations that followed.

PRAYER: Heavenly Father, may we make even greater room in our hearts for your Son, our Solid Rock, that we may remain firm amidst the sinking sands of the world. In Jesus' name. Amen.

THOUGHT: Are you standing on the Rock?

47. 'TIS SO SWEET TO TRUST IN JESUS

"That we should be to the praise of his glory, who first trusted in Christ." (EPHESIANS 1:12)

One of the best loved hymns of trust and faith was written after a beach picnic that turned into a tragedy. It was a beautiful morning and plans were made for a day's outing at a nearby beach. Louisa M. Stead (1859-1917) soon prepared lunch for her husband, her four year old daughter, Lily, and herself and then left for the warm sands of a Long Island beach. Louisa had a chance to count her many blessings as Lily made sand houses and her husband relaxed beside her. Suddenly her thoughts were interrupted by the cries of a boy struggling desperately in the water. Without any hesitation Mr. Stead took off his outer garments and went to the boy's rescue. By this time the boy had become panic stricken and when his would-be rescuer reached his side the frightened boy grabbed him with a vise-like grip. Some progress was made toward shore, but soon both disappeared beneath the waves. All Louisa could do was to clutch Lily to her and watch in horror as neither man nor boy appeared again.

The weeks that passed were difficult and lonely as this frail and grief-stricken woman, who wanted to be a missionary, leaned more heavily upon Jesus. As a young woman she had gone to the altar and dedicated her life to the Lord as a missionary. However, she was not physically able to meet the requirements but her missionary zeal never waned. It was not until years later that her life-long desire was realized. Ten years after the tragedy at the beach she remarried. This time it was to a missionary and they served for many years in South Africa and Southern Rhodesia.

It was during those heart-breaking months following her first husband's death that she wrote the words to the heart warming hymn, " 'Tis So Sweet to Trust in Jesus."

'Tis so sweet to trust in Jesus
  Just to take Him at His word;
Just to rest upon His promise;
  Just to know, "Thus saith the Lord."

* * * * * * *

John Patton and his young wife were among the earliest missionaries of the church. They went to the New Hebrides where some of the natives were still cannibals. They were the only white people and the only Christians there. Their work was not easy, but they were happy in their love for each other. The year after their arrival a son was born and their hearts were filled with joy. That joy soon vanished for death came and took both the wife and child. John Patton told how he dug a grave and laid his loved ones there. Then he adds these significant and touching words. "If it had not been for Jesus . . . I would have gone mad and died before that lonely grave."

It is Jesus who gives hope to our troubled hearts. That is why we need Him every hour. Whatever your burden or heartache at this moment, lean hard upon Jesus. He is your greatest need. Take Him at His word and believe. Whatever your problem trust Him for the answer.

PRAYER: We are thankful, our Father, that we can trust in Jesus no matter what may come. You planned it that way so that we can lean upon your Son for our strength when life tumbles in. In Jesus' name. Amen.

THOUGHT: There is no new sorrow. We will never be called upon to bear anything that was not borne before.

48. IT IS WELL WITH MY SOUL

"He satisfieth the longing soul, and filleth the hungry soul with goodness." (PSALM 107:9)

Horatio Gates Stafford (1828-1888), a lawyer, was too busy to sail with his wife and four young children to Europe on the *S.S. Ville du Havre.* He had lost all his possessions in the Chicago fire of 1871 and since that time had worked relentlessly to recoup his losses. Now, two years later, he felt the time had come for his wife and children to have a vacation. He would join them on the completion of his present work in Chicago. He went with them to New York, and watched on November 15, 1873, as the luxury liner left on her overseas voyage.

Although the steamer had encountered rough seas at the beginning of her trip, the weather had moderated as she drew closer to France. On Friday, November 21, even the fog had lifted and everyone was happy and certain of a safe journey the rest of the way. One of the passengers wrote, "The night was clear and starry, the sea smooth – what had we now to fear?" At two o'clock the next morning, however, that peaceful scene suddenly changed. The seaman on the bow watch was startled to see the large English iron sailing vessel, *Lochearn,* bearing down upon them. Straight for the *Ville du Havre* it came, never slackening speed or changing direction. The damage was so great that only sixteen minutes elapsed before the luxury steamer vanished from sight, carrying with her 226 passengers and crew including the four Stafford children. Nine days later, when the 87 survivors arrived at Cardiff, Wales, the heartbroken mother sent this cable to her husband: "Saved alone."

Horatio Stafford, who had already lost so much in the Chicago holocaust, had now lost the four girls whom he adored. He immediately made arrangements to meet his wife, taking the first vessel going in that direction. Slightly west of the Azores, he was shown the spot where the *Ville du Havre* sank. The next day, struggling to control his tears, he wrote:

When peace like a river attendeth my way,
When sorrows like sea billows roll,
Whatever my lot, Thou hast taught me to say,
"It is well, it is well with my soul!"

* * * * * * *

Is it well with your soul and mine? Do we love Christ now just as much as when we joined the church? Does He mean the same to us as He did when some loved one was near death's door and we prayed so fervently that he be spared? Is He just as real to us at present as when we were on our own bed of sickness, not knowing what the next hour would bring? We thought a lot of Him then – do we think the same of Him now? Is there still the thrill of joy in our lives at the name of Jesus? Do we still have that feeling of giving ourselves in service to Him as when we first dedicated our lives to Him? Is it really well with our souls?

PRAYER: O Lord, help me to make an honest appraisal of my life, that I may ascertain how healthy I am spiritually. In Jesus' name. Amen.

THOUGHT: Unless Christ is the center of our lives, it is not well with our souls.

49. BLESSED ASSURANCE

"And when they had lifted up their eyes, they saw no man, save Jesus only." (MATTHEW 17:8)

Hymn poems and tunes are joined together in many ways. The usual process is for the author of a poem to seek a composer. It was the reverse when Mrs. Joseph Knapp came to Fanny Crosby (1820-1915) with a melody she had recently finished. She played the music through several times and then asked, "Fanny, what does this tune suggest to you?" The blind hymn writer who had listened intently to the music, immediately responded, "To me it means 'Blessed Assurance, Jesus is Mine'." On that day in 1873, Fanny began to write the words that have blessed millions ever since.

Miss Crosby was always happy in spite of her blindness, and

scattered sunshine wherever she went. She was welcomed everywhere and enjoyed the friendship of presidents and other leaders in government as well as church leaders who went to her for advice or with suggestions regarding the writing of another hymn. Never once did she allow her lack of sight to depress her regardless of the many problems she faced.

When she was eight years old she wrote a poem, the second verse indicating her determination to rise above her handicap.

How many blessings I enjoy,
  That other people don't.
To weep and sigh because I'm blind,
  I cannot, and I won't.

"In my quiet moments," she said, "I say to myself, 'Fanny, there are many worse things than blindness that might happen to you. The loss of the mind is a thousand times worse than the loss of the eyes.' " This is an example of the optimistic attitude she carried through her long life.

Blessed Assurance, Jesus is mine!
  O what a foretaste of glory divine!
Heir of salvation, purchase of God,
  Born of His Spirit, washed in His blood.

* * * * * * *

Speaking at the Florida Chain of Missions some years ago, an Episcopal Church home missionary told of a letter he received from a Dakota Indian co-worker. The writer described the effect the television wild west programs had upon his children. As he watched he observed how fascinated they were by an early pioneer wagon train surrounded by Indians. There seemed no hope for the settlers and each child sat, tense and still, on the edge of his seat. Just at the right moment the United States Army appeared, saving the pioneers and inflicting great punishment upon the attackers. Immediately his children, though Indians, began to wildly cheer and applaud. Then the letter writer added, "Captain Jones, my children do not know who they are."

Do we as Christians know who we are? In a world often hostile to the Gospel, do we make it clear that we have been with Jesus? No matter how enticing some things are, may we never forget the prior claim Jesus has on our lives. Fanny Crosby knew to whom she belonged. In the third verse of the above hymn, she writes, "I in my

Savior am happy and blest." That should be the source of our happiness also.

PRAYER: Dear Lord, help us to remember the suffering and sacrifice that has made our Christian heritage possible. May we rejoice in the realization that we belong to you. Amen.

THOUGHT: If we belong to Jesus we will have no trouble remembering who we are.

50. MY JESUS, AS THOU WILT

"Oh my Father, if it is possible, let this cup pass from me: nevertheless not as I will, but as thou wilt." (MATTHEW 26:39)

Benjamin Schmolke (1672-1737) was one of the most prolific hymn writers of Germany, having produced over nine hundred hymns. Yet his life was filled with tragedy. He became a Lutheran pastor and was appointed to the church at Schweidnitz in 1702. Later, during the counter-Reformation, all the Lutheran churches in that area were closed. The main church had to be built outside the city walls and be without a tower or bells. He could not even serve communion to a sick parishioner without permission. This was the only church permitted to serve the people of thirty-six villages, and the work became so exhausting that Schmolke's health failed.

This hymn, like so many others, came out of a tragic and sad situation. Schmolke's home town was nearly destroyed by fire and two of his children died in the flames. He suffered a stroke, lost the use of his right hand and eventually became blind. He refused to give up and preached another five years until other strokes led to his death. He never lost his faith and during those sorrow-filled years kept writing hymns of trust and confidence.

My Jesus, as Thou wilt,
  O may Thy will be mine!
Into Thy hand of love
  I will my all resign.
Through sorrow or through joy,
  Conduct me as Thine own
And help me still to say,
  "My Lord, Thy will be done!"

* * * * * * *

One day while visiting a member of my parish a little fellow from across the street stopped me and began to ask questions. He was only five years old and his playmates told him I was a minister. He had never talked with a minister before and the questions he asked were amazing. I explained about God, Jesus and the church. After I had finished he said, "I want to go to Sunday School and learn more." I think he would have asked questions all afternoon had he not been led away by his playmates.

That was in the summer. Six months later his mother and father came home in the early hours of the morning in a drunken and stupid condition, which was a common occurrence. They had to smoke before they went to bed and became careless with their matches and set fire to the house. They never thought of anything else but saving themselves and when the fire was finally extinguished that little boy was found burned to death in his bed. A few said it was God's will, but not me. At the funeral service I did not read the usual words said at that time, "The Lord gave and the Lord hath taken away." It was drunken parents and not the Lord who took away the life of that little boy. Jesus said, "It is not the will of your Father in heaven that one of these little ones should perish." Yet they are perishing continually because of the sins of parents.

PRAYER: Father, help us to distinguish between your will and the destruction man brings upon life. We are thankful that your will is always for our good. In Jesus' name. Amen.

THOUGHT: God's will is not something to endure, but something to do.

51. I WILL SING OF MY REDEEMER

"Who gave himself for us, that he might redeem us from all iniquity, and purify unto himself a peculiar people, zealous of good works." (Titus 2:14)

A hymn that thrilled my heart as a teenager was, "I Will Sing of My Redeemer." I had no idea of the tragedy behind the hymn or the sorrow it caused the Christian world of that day. It concerned one of the greatest hymn composers of all time who died while still in the prime of life.

Philip Bliss (1838-1876) who wrote some of our best known hymns and composed the music for many more, took time off from his work at the Moody Tabernacle in December, 1876, in order that he and his wife might visit his aged mother in Buffalo, New York. They had an enjoyable visit which brought great comfort to his mother. The train on which they were to return to Chicago had to cross over a high bridge in Ashtabula, Ohio. The snowstorm that had started earlier had worsened. Halfway across the bridge the headlights of another engine approaching them were seen and a terrible crash soon followed. The train caught fire from the broken stove and plunged into the river below. Under the weight of both trains the bridge had collapsed.

Ninety-two passengers lost their lives, including Mr. and Mrs. Philip Bliss. It is said that Bliss was thrown clear but not seeing his wife he went back into the flaming wreckage and died with her. He was only thirty-eight years old. Several days later his trunk arrived on another train and in it was found the last hymn-poem he had written. The title was, "I Will Sing of My Redeemer!" He probably had a tune already to put on paper when he arrived home, but it was another composer, James McGranahan, who eventually added the music to the poem.

I will sing of my Redeemer
And His wondrous love to me;
On the cruel cross He suffered
From the curse He set me free.

* * * * * * *

One of our ordained women ministers in South America, speaking in the Upper Room Chapel, told of an experience that was hers while at Scarritt. It concerned a black custodian who very early each winter morning took care of the furnace in the houses where the students lived. Almost always she could hear him singing, "I want to be like Jesus in my heart." She said, "He and I were very different. I was comfortable. I did not have to do the type of work he did. He did not have the opportunities the church had given me through the years. But we had one thing in common. We both wanted to be like Jesus."

That should be our desire too. This custodian loved to sing about his Redeemer. He yearned to be like Jesus.

PRAYER: Thank you, O God, for sending your Son into the world to redeem us and give us a freedom which the world can never give. In Jesus' name. Amen.

THOUGHT: It is not enough for others to hear that we are Christian. That which is essential is that they see in us the Master's spirit.

52. JUST A CLOSER WALK WITH THEE

"As ye have therefore received Christ Jesus the Lord, so walk ye in Him." (COLOSSIANS 2:6)

I have in my possession a large volume entitled, "Worship Resources for the Christian Year." A number of my poems are included, but underneath one, instead of my name is the word "anon." In fact, someone even added an extra verse. I don't object to the verse because it is well written. What I object to is the word "anon," not only here but attached to any poem or hymn. It is amazing how often the author or composer of some of our best loved hymns is unknown.

One of our most often used sacred songs was written by an author whose name is not recorded. This is nothing new. Some of the hymns we sing regularly were treated in the same manner. Dr. John Rippon's song book published in 1787 is designated only by the letter "K." Dr. Rippon claimed his hymns were by the best authors but he was not concerned about always including their names. "How Firm a Foundation" is one of the anonymous hymns in that "Selection."

Another more recent song, "Just a Closer Walk with Thee," is in the same category. This is a heart warming piece and is sung by most denominations. The author is designated either as "anon," "Negro Spiritual" or "Source unknown," depending upon the hymn book in which it appears. The words are set to a traditional spiritual melody. The chorus follows.

Just a closer walk with Thee,
Grant it, Jesus, is my plea;
Daily walking close to Thee,
Let it be, dear Lord, let it be.

* * * * * * *

One wintry morning, five year old Dianne stood gazing out from our parsonage window. She was deep in thought as she surveyed the landscape. Soon she became disturbed. Turning a serious face toward her mother, she asked, "Mommie, what would happen if Jesus came today?" She was thinking of the many pictures of Jesus in which He was always barefoot. She was concerned as she thought about Christ coming to the north country of New Hampshire in zero weather, with snow everywhere. Finally, with the same deep concern, she asked, "Mommie, do you think Jesus' feet could fit into Daddy's shoes?"

I was greatly humbled when later informed of this incident. I asked myself, "Am I allowing Jesus to walk in my shoes? Have I given Him control of my possessions, my tongue, my desires, my life? Do those who see me and listen to my words catch a vision of Him?" These are the questions we should all ask ourselves.

PRAYER: We want to walk close to You, our Saviour, for our bitter experiences have taught us the folly of leaving You and attempting to go it alone. Draw us closer that the joy of that fellowship may ever be ours. In the precious Name of Jesus. Amen.

THOUGHT: "Do I allow Jesus to walk in my shoes?" Our life will be blessed indeed if we can answer, "Yes."

53. PASS ME NOT, O GENTLE SAVIOUR

"*. . . Jesus of Nazareth passeth by.*" (LUKE 18:37)

The sweetest voice of the past generation was not that of Jenny Lind but Fanny J. Crosby (1820-1915) who wrote 7,000 hymns. Seldom does a Sunday pass without the singing of one of her hymns. What made the voice of this gentle woman so sweet? It was her perpetual night of blindness that was illuminated by the touch of Jesus upon her life. She lost her sight when only six weeks old due to the incompetency of those who attended her.

She wrote her first poem before the age of ten. It was about that time she dedicated her life to Christ and asked Him to make her useful in spite of her blindness. Though she wrote poetry at this early age, she did not write her first hymn until her midforties.

Composers of sacred music often came to Fanny for a hymn-poem that would fit their tune. William H. Doane, however, didn't yet have a melody, but he had one line of a possible poem that he was unable to banish from his mind. He needed someone to develop his thoughts into a hymn after which he would compose the music, and the person he knew to be best fitted for that responsibility was Fanny Crosby. When that poem was finished he knew he had a hymn that would appeal to all seekers after the Lord, and he prayerfully prepared to set it to the most heart-stirring music he could compose. The fact that both the poet and composer were successful in this endeavor was immediately evident.

Fanny describes this event in the following few words. "My hymn which first won worldwide attention was, 'Pass Me Not, O Gentle Saviour.' Mr. W. H. Doane, who became a very dear friend of mine, suggested the subject to me. It was written in the year 1868."

Pass me not, O gentle Saviour,
  Hear my humble cry;
While on others thou art calling,
  Do not pass me by.

* * * * * * *

When Jesus touches us we know it. He touched my life when I was 17 years old. I was president of an athletic club in Boston and my church was having revival services. The pastor asked me to attend. I reluctantly consented and persuaded most of the other club members to go with me. We completely filled one pew. Who preached, I do not know. What was said I can't remember. I was thinking of the much needed practice for our next game that we were missing. Suddenly I was jolted out of my thoughts by something that was happening within me. The Lord wanted me there that night, and sometime during that service He stopped before my pew, touched me and called my name. I bounced from my seat and went to the altar. The rest of the fellows stared at me as if I had lost my mind. Such was not the case, for at that altar I not only dedicated my life to Christ but also to the ministry. It was indeed a touch that made me whole.

PRAYER: Touch us again, Lord! One touch is not enough. It is too easy for that blaze to diminish; for our first love to wane. We need your touch repeatedly that this sacred flame may continue to glow. In your dear name we pray. Amen.

THOUGHT: When Jesus touches our lives we will know it, because from that time on we will never be the same.

54. MY JESUS, I LOVE THEE

"Lord, Thou knowest all things; thou knowest that I love thee." (JOHN 21:17)

Dr. Adoniram Judson Gordon, pastor of the Clarendon Street Church, Boston, had just found in a London hymn book an anonymous hymn entitled, "My Jesus, I Love Thee." It was later discovered that these words were written by a young man, William Ralph Featherstone (1846-1873) who lived to be only twenty-seven years old.

Dr. Gordon was probably never aware of the identity of the author, but he liked what was written. It was the tune he disliked. He was certain that these soul-searching words would never live unless the music was changed. The doctor had already spent five years preparing a hymnal, much of that time in meditation and prayer, humming to himself every new hymn that came to his attention. As these words came constantly before his mind, he began to concentrate on the proper music to fit them. During an hour spent in prayer and meditation the inspiration suddenly came and he started to hum the tune that was then forming in his mind. He knew he had it, and to the words he considered anonymous he added the beautiful melody to which it has since been sung.

My Jesus, I love Thee, I know Thou art mine.
For Thee all the follies of sin I resign.
My gracious redeemer, my Saviour art Thou;
If ever I loved Thee, my Jesus, 'tis now.

* * * * * * *

It is said that when Gustave Dore had nearly completed one of his faces of Jesus, a woman stepped into his studio very quietly, and was unnoticed by him. She stood gazing with admiration on the painting. When the artist became aware of her presence he said, "Pardon me, Madam, I did not know that you were here." In reply she pointed to the face of Jesus and said, "You must love Him very much to be able to paint Him so."

"Love Him, madam," replied the great painter, "I should think I do love Him, but if I loved Him more I would paint Him better."

Is not that the trouble with us? We love Him to a certain extent, but if we loved Him more we would follow Him more closely. We would be willing to step out of the crowd and answer, "Yes" to His beckoning. If we loved Him more we would be willing to deny self, take up the cross and follow wherever He would lead.

PRAYER: Our Father, may we never be ashamed to talk about You. Give us wisdom and tact as we present Your Son to a world yearning for someone in whom they can put their trust. In Jesus' name. Amen.

THOUGHT: A Christian is a person in love with Christ.

55. O LOVE THAT WILT NOT LET ME GO

"Having loved His own which were in the world, He loved them unto the end." (JOHN 13:1)

The usually carefree student was depressed but determined not to panic. His studies were good in spite of his failing eyesight. Even at fifteen he knew that it was only a matter of time before he would be blind. Instead of giving up his attempt for an education that information only spurred him on to greater endeavor. He enrolled in the University of Glasgow, Scotland, graduating at the age of nineteen. To be a minister of the Gospel was his desire and much of his work was done in total darkness.

His one source of comfort was in knowing that he would soon be married. He had been engaged for some time to an attractive young woman who apparently was not aware that he would lose his sight completely. However, she had to know, so he explained to her just what the doctor had told him. Her reaction was not slow in coming. She broke off her engagement, later saying that she could not go through life chained to a blind man. This was the second crushing blow that came to George Matheson (1842-1906) within the short span of a few years. Not even the love of his sisters, who helped him in his studies could heal his broken heart. As a result of this double tragedy he leaned more heavily upon Jesus whose love he knew was unfailing.

It was this experience, no doubt, that at the age of forty led him to write his inspiring hymn of faith and trust. "My hymn," he said, "was composed in the manse of Innellan on the evening of June 6, 1882. I was at that time alone. It was the day of my sister's marriage, and the rest of the family were staying overnight in Glasgow. Something had happened to me, which was known only to myself, and which caused the most severe mental suffering. The writing of the hymn was the quickest bit of work I ever did in my life. I had the impression of having it dictated to me by some inward voice rather than of working it out myself."

O Love that wilt not let me go,
  I rest my weary soul in Thee:
I give Thee back the life I owe,
  That in Thine ocean depths its flow
May richer, fuller be.

* * * * * * *

Some years ago a ship from Africa docked in America. Among those on board were two men with completely different backgrounds. One was Theodore Roosevelt, then president of the United States, just returning from a lion hunt. The other was a missionary, broken in health because of his long years of service among fierce tribesmen. Multitudes were on hand to greet the president. Bands played and crowds cheered. But no one was there to welcome the frail missionary. Momentarily loneliness overtook him and leaning against the rail for support he prayed, "Dear Lord, I've given my life to save men. The president has been shooting lions. We both came home on the same ship and crowds welcome him, but there is none to welcome me." At that moment God spoke to him and said, "But son, you're not home yet."

The next time we complain of our problems, whether pain, sorrow or disappointment, let us also remember that we are not home yet. We will face trials, difficult situations and sometimes lonely hours, but we haven't reached our destination. We are only on the way. Like Matheson, therefore, let us draw closer to the One whose love will not let us go.

PRAYER: Our Father, when darkness descends upon us, may we remember that our Saviour is not only the Light of the world, but is also He who lights up our life. In the Master's name. Amen.

THOUGHT: When lights suddenly grow dim we need the readjustments the Master gives.

56. I SURRENDER ALL

"He saith unto them, Follow me, and I will make you fishers of men." (MATTHEW 4:19)

A hymn often used for an altar call is, "I Surrender All." It was written by a former school supervisor who later became an evangelist. This change was not a spur of the moment event, but something he wrestled with long and earnestly. He liked his work and he also liked art. In fact the latter became an obsession with him. More than that, however, there was money in it. He was a successful amateur artist as well as a happy, satisfied supervisor. It is easy to see how Judson W. Van De Venter (1855-1939) would be content with his life style. God, however, who was aware of his ability, continued to hound him. Van De Venter was a good churchman, faithful to every responsibility placed upon him.

Things went along as usual until a series of evangelistic services were held in his church. He became actively engaged in counselling and personal work that week. He had done this before but never with the feeling he was experiencing now. He knew the Lord was very close to him, urging him to engage in some form of Christian service. His friends, who were aware of his ability and now beheld his deeper consecration, encouraged him to give up his teaching and use his wonderful talents for the Lord. His teaching didn't cause him to waver in his desire to do religious work, but his art did. He still had visions of becoming a recognized artist. Eventually the Lord won and Van De Venter was ordained and in time became a much sought after evangelist. He said of that experience, "At last the pivotal hour of my life came and I surrendered all." He also said that God had "hidden a song in his heart" and one of those hidden songs came pouring forth from his life in 1895, after he made that important surrender of his life.

All to Jesus I surrender
All to Him I freely give;
I will ever love and trust Him,
In His presence daily live.

* * * * * * *

When the late Edgar J. Helms, founder of the Goodwill Industries was seventeen, he left home to attend Cornell College. He rode the fifty miles to the nearest depot on a slow horse drawn vehicle with his pastor. At the urging of the minister he attended a camp meeting service on the way. He considered it the dullest hour he ever spent. The night was cold and wet, and to his youthful mind, the meeting was just as deadening. He was about to leave when the speaker made the prediction that someone present would be converted, who would later lead thousands to Christ. "The conviction gripped me," he said, "that this reference was to me." Before retiring that night he knelt beside a tree and prayed. When he awoke the next morning he experienced an indescribable peace. From that moment his desire was to become a minister that he might fulfill the mission he was certain God had in mind for him.

The Lord has a mission for every life. He wanted His disciples to be fishers of men. He needed Judson Van De Venter to be an evangelist. He wanted Dr. Helms for work among the neglected poor of the cities. As a result, this youth turned his back upon the study of law and prepared himself for the ministry.

PRAYER: Our Father, lead us in the pathway of service that we may be more alert to the needs of others. Help us to trust You, especially if that place appears difficult and unpromising. In Jesus' name. Amen.

THOUGHT: To follow Jesus means to serve where He would serve, love as He would love, and live as He would live.

57. O MASTER, LET ME WALK WITH THEE

"He that sayeth he abideth in Him ought himself also to walk, even as He walked." (I JOHN 2:6)

He was a courageous man, a crusader for right and was always in trouble. He was in serious trouble with his own denomination when he criticised them for accepting money he considered "tainted." In his earlier years before attending Williams College, Washington Gladden (1836-1918) worked as a printer and it was at this trade that he became interested in writing.

During his pastorate at the Congregational Church in Springfield, Massachusetts, he was the editor of a weekly paper called "Sunday Afternoon." One department of that paper was known as the "Still Hour," which consisted of religious subjects. In one of the March, 1897 issues, appeared the poem, "O Master, Let Me Walk with Thee." He wrote it as a meditation and not as a hymn. He had been preaching on labor management problems in his Sunday evening services, which aroused many of his wealthy and influential leaders. "Your job is to save souls," they shouted, "and not to regulate business." He turned for encouragement to his brother pastors but they silently withdrew from his presence. It was with a heavy heart, because of the misunderstanding and hatred of those who opposed his views, that he began to put his thoughts on paper. The second stanza of the original poem was left out of the hymn because it was considered unsuitable for church worship, but the words help us to understand his mood and his determination to live above the taunts of men. Two of those lines follow.

"Help me to bear the sting of spite;
The hate of men who hide thy light."

Dr. Gladden was an outstanding minister and leader of his denomination. Over thirty books testify to the amount of writing that came from his pen. Although he wrote many poems he did not consider himself a hymn writer. He was perhaps the most surprised when this poem was taken from the "Sunday Afternoon" magazine and made into a hymn when H. Percy Smith composed the music to which it is sung.

O Master, let me walk with Thee
In lowly paths of service free;
Tell me Thy secret; help me to bear
The strain of toil, the fret of care.

* * * * * * *

When the pastor of my youth, Dr. Edgar J. Helms, founded the Goodwill Industries through his work in the South End of Boston, he was carrying out the Lord's mandate to be of service to the least of these. He has been with the Master for many years but his work lives on in every section of our country.

Washington Gladden wanted to walk with the Master in lowly paths of service wherever those paths led. This should be our desire also and those paths multiply with every passing year.

PRAYER: O Master, we do want to walk with you. Wherever you would go, we want to go, and whatever you would do, we want to do. Grant that we may measure up to your expectations that this desire may be fulfilled. Amen.

THOUGHT: No one can follow Jesus without becoming like him.

58. O GALILEE, SWEET GALILEE

"Jesus departed from thence, and came nigh unto the Sea of Galilee, and went up into a mountain, and sat there." (MATTHEW 15:29)

Not every archaeologist to the Holy Land was content with merely digging and studying the results. Some received a vision that remained with them and caused them to bless the world with their writings. Some of our most precious hymns and sacred songs came from such devout souls. Dr. Robert Morris (1818-1888) gave us such a hymn. During a lull in his work he began to trace the steps of Jesus.

Morris had been commissioned to go to Palestine in 1868 on an historic and archaeological mission. Always with reverent steps, he explored areas of Jewish and Christian beginnings. His great desire was to walk where Jesus walked, recalling the events that occurred at each place. While sitting above the ruins of the supposed site of Capernaum he began to write a poem. Every thing he saw and every sound he heard took Morris back to Galilee and the One who ministered there. When the poem was finished he sent it to his friend Horatio R. Palmer, one of America's finest composers of sacred music. Palmer later said that the poem remained in his thoughts until "it floated out in the melody you know." We know the hymn as "Oh, Galilee, Sweet Galilee."

Oh, Galilee, Sweet Galilee,
  Where Jesus loved so much to be;
Oh, Galilee, blue Galilee,
  Come sing thy song again to me.

* * * * * * *

Have you been in the presence of the Lord today? Have you seen Him; have you talked with Him? If so, what has His presence done for your life? You can still have that Galilean experience. You can still hear His voice as He speaks to your soul. Every place of dedication can be your Galilee, the spot where you have met Jesus and your life has been changed.

The altar where I dedicated my life to Jesus and the ministry is no more. The church has been torn down to make way for a super highway. But at that altar I met the Christ of Galilee and He called me, and praise the Lord, without hesitation I followed Him. You can do the same.

Now that this experience has taken place, let us go forward. Let us not continue to stall or be content to stand still. The Kingdom can't tarry. It must go forward. Let us go further in our devotion to Him; further in our dedication, in our service, our giving to the church and our response to its program. Jesus never held back and neither should we. Let us go forth and take our place beside Him.

PRAYER: Heavenly Father, we are thankful for the many places of dedication you have provided for us. When we have failed You have made it possible to begin again. Thank You. In Jesus' name. Amen.

THOUGHT: The second birth is the place where God puts our sins behind Him and forgets them.

59. COME, YE SINNERS, POOR AND NEEDY

"I came not to call the righteous, but sinners to repentance." (LUKE 5:32)

It saddens one to find well trained spiritual individuals suddenly turning their backs upon the warm faith they once professed. Joseph Hart (1712-1768) is an example. He was raised in a Christian home, only, later in life, to become an atheist. He was liberally educated and considered deeply spiritual, but the day came when following Jesus lost its luster. In the beginning of his worldly endeavors he began to indulge in evil practices that he once despised. After the thrill of this departed he began to condemn Christianity. Eventually he was no longer content to speak against his former faith, but he denounced it and all religions in writing. He still was not satisfied so he began to translate the slanderous writings of others. For some time he had been shunned by former friends; now he was not welcomed anywhere. Even the non-churchgoers refused to associate with one they called an infidel. He became such a nuisance that one town compelled him to leave so he returned to London. While there he entered a Moravian chapel to criticize and condemn. He never did either. The message of the preacher so gripped him he could hardly wait to get home to seek forgiveness. Upon reaching the place of his abode, he fell upon his knees and yielded his life once again to the Lord. Immediately he found a weight lifted from his shoulders. From that moment on he began to write—not the condemning pamphlets of the past, but Christian hymns.

It was now Holy Week, 1767, and the thought of Christ suffering upon the cross for his sins, created in him a heart-warming experience. He had been ordained a Congregational minister seven years before but this Holy Week experience caused him to write:

Come, ye sinners, poor and needy,
  Weak and wounded, sick and sore;
Jesus ready stands to save you,
  Full of pity, love, and power;
He is able, He is able,
  He is willing; doubt no more.

This was the story of his own experience. He had to share it with others.

* * * * * * *

A policeman directing traffic in one of our cities, was accustomed to shouting to anyone who crossed without his signal. One day a citizen took him to task for what he termed his rudeness. Without taking his eyes off the traffic the policeman replied, "Mister, I've saved three lives already this morning. How many have you saved?"

Are there any among us who does not have something to be saved from? Are we all that pure and clean? There is no perfect life but one, and He was crucified nearly 2000 years ago. The rest of us have faults, weaknesses, and our little pet sins. Why should we keep holding onto them when one step will take us to Him who can remove these unwanted sins from our life forever.

PRAYER: Oh, Our Father, save us from the sins that so easily beset us. May we see clearly that though they might not be sins of the flesh they still can condemn us. May we see clearly our wrong doings that by your help we can cast them from us. In Jesus' name. Amen.

THOUGHT: The touch of the Master can bring life to anyone.

60. MY GOD, MY FATHER, WHILE I STRAY

"Be of good courage, and He shall strengthen your heart, all ye that hope in the Lord." (PSALM 31:24)

For over fifty years Charlotte Elliott (1789-1871) was an invalid. She did not dwell upon her condition even though she yearned at times to be able to do what others were doing. "Even in the vale of suffering," she wrote, "there are blessed companions to associate with, sweet consolations to partake of, heavenly privileges to enjoy." There is certainly no sign of self-pity in these words. Instead, her sincere spiritual life not only brought comfort to her, but through her writings, to others. As a young woman she was at times irritable, but during her long period of illness she was known for her sunny disposition. Her hymns were sent forth to help others in their suffering. The hymn that won a place for her in the hearts of multitudes, is the autobiography of her own life, "Just as I Am," and this inspiring piece has led to unnumbered conversions through the years.

One of her first hymns was that of resignation, an acceptance of her physical condition. It was published with many of her other hymns in 1834, under the title of "The Invalid's Hymn Book." In this little volume appeared the hymn for this meditation, "My God, My Father, while I Stray." It illustrates the physical difficulty she faced, yet through it all resigning herself to God's will. She wrote, "How many hard struggles and apparently fruitless ones, has it cost me to become resigned to this appointment of my Heavenly Father! But the struggle is now over." She was a courageous woman. The second verse of this hymn reveals a little of that struggle together with the victory that followed.

It has been sung through the years to the tune Hanford, composed by Arthur S. Sullivan.

Though dark my path, and sad my lot,
Let me be still and murmur not,
Or breathe the prayer divinely taught,
"Thy will be done!"

* * * * * * *

In my early ministry, I had as a member of my church, one of the last chanty-men of the old sailing ship days. This office was considered the most desirable berth a sailor could obtain. There was a lively song for every major activity aboard ship and the chanty-man had to know them all. His duty was to sing that he might keep the courage of the toiling men from waning.

Clipper ships and chanty-men have gone but the need of courage is ever present. No one is really prepared for the future unless he possesses the courageous spirit of Christ. It was He who brought courage to those who faced the upheavals of His day. It was He who quieted His faint hearted disciples with the words, "Be of good cheer," and later reminded His heroic but often oppressed followers, that He would be with them always.

PRAYER: Our Father, may we possess the courage of your Son, that we too, may face the problems of our world serenely and with confidence. May it be our desire to help keep the courage of others from waning. In Jesus' name. Amen.

THOUGHT: Jesus is still the way to courageous living.

61. I NEED THEE EVERY HOUR

"Let us therefore come boldly unto the throne of grace, that we may obtain mercy and find grace to help in time of need." (Hebrews 4:16)

The Rev. Robert Lowry composed music for a large number of deeply spiritual hymns. While pastor of the Hanson Place Baptist Church, Brooklyn, N. Y., he discovered that one of his parishioners, Mrs. Annie Hawks (1835-1918) had written some fine poems. He encouraged her to write others that could be used as hymns. Although she did not consider herself fully qualified for such an undertaking she decided she would follow his advice.

One day in June 1872, as Annie was going about her household duties the thought came to her, "How could anyone live without Jesus? How could they face the trials, temptations and sorrow that come to every life?" At the moment she was enjoying a healthy, happy life. All of her material needs were met. She possessed a great faith. She was happily married and loved her home. Then she began to think of those not so fortunate. Their needs must be great, she decided. She then wondered what would happen if she was not so blessed. Suddenly she felt the nearness of the Master and immediately sat down to write "I Need Thee every Hour."

After finishing the poem, she read it over several times, and wondered if she dared show it to Dr. Lowry. He had asked her to bring to him every poem but this was such a simple piece, she was not sure it was worth bothering with. When her composer friend later read it he saw something in the poem that she had not seen. He realized that these words were words that would stir the hearts of multitudes the world over. Annie had not written a chorus, so sitting at the organ he composed the soul-stirring music of the verse, and added words and music for a chorus of the heart warming hymn.

Annie Hawks had no idea of what her hymn meant to others until her husband died sixteen years later. She lived to be 82 years old and the hymn that gave her the greatest comfort through those many years was her own.

I need Thee every hour, Most gracious Lord;
No tender voice like Thine, Can peace afford.
  I need Thee, O I need Thee,
  Every hour I need Thee;
  O bless me now, my Saviour,
  I come to Thee!

* * * * * * *

We are always in need of Jesus. We cannot leave Him in a closed church when the worship service is over. A stained glass window depicting Christ is beautiful, but the Master is not content to stay in a stained glass window. He who walks the highways of life proclaiming the eternal message of God's love, does not want to stay in a window in a locked church.

Neither can we leave Him at home when we go forth to face the problems of another busy week. What is there to remind us of His spirit in the impatience of the drivers who like us, are hurrying on their way? Are we reminded of Christ in our place of employment? Does the conversation around us daily provide the inspiration we need? And for those who stay at home, is Jesus any more real at the close of a day after they have listened to their favorite television program or finished their household duties?

Of course Jesus is with us wherever we go. We cannot leave Him in church or at our place of business or at home, but if we do not feel the need of Him each day it is equivalent to locking Him out of our life.

PRAYER: You are, O Christ, our Great Companion. We remember your blessed promise, "Lo, I am with you always," and it gives us comfort, for it reminds us that we do not walk life's road alone. Thank you for your presence and your love. Amen.

THOUGHT: Some people leave Jesus the moment the need of Him is greatest.

62. MY FAITH LOOKS UP TO THEE

"And the apostles said unto the Lord, Increase our faith." (LUKE 17:5)

He wrote one of our best loved hymns when he was only twenty-two years old. Yet he didn't intend it to be a hymn. He wrote the poem for his own comfort during a time of great stress. He was overwhelmed at the time by both illness and poverty.

He had previously graduated from Phillips Andover Academy in Massachusetts and Yale, and was now teaching in New York City. He never intended teaching to be his life's work. His desire was to be a clergyman, and he realized that the only way to achieve that goal was to teach and study theology at the same time. This was no easy assignment and he spent many long, frustrating hours each day to accomplish his purpose. It was while carrying this burden in the winter of 1830 that Ray Palmer (1808-1887) decided to write a poem that would express his innermost feelings. He had no thought of writing it for others to see.

He later said that it was with little effort that he wrote the stanzas but they were penned with great feeling. "I wrote," he said, "with very tender emotion and ended the last line with tears. I composed them with a deep consciousness of my own needs, with not the slightest thought of writing for another eye, and the least of all of writing a hymn for Christian worship."

In 1835, Ray Palmer, the son of Judge Thomas Palmer of Rhode Island, became a Congregational minister and served churches in Maine and New York before becoming corresponding secretary of the American Congregational Union.

My faith looks up to Thee,
  Thou Lamb of Calvary,
Saviour Divine!

Now hear me while I pray,
Take all my guilt away,
O, Let me from this day
Be wholly thine!

* * * * * * *

Upon receiving a call that a friend was anxious to see me, I hastened to his home. He had lost a leg a few years before and had been an invalid since. That day he had fallen from his wheelchair and injured the other leg. When I entered his bedroom he kept repeating, "Something is missing, something is missing." When I asked what it was, he replied, "My faith; it is gone; I don't have it any more; I've lost it." As he spoke he smote his breast and the tears coursed down his cheeks. Looking upon his distress, I realized that the loss of faith to this devout man was a greater calamity than the loss of his leg.

As I left I began to question my faith, wondering whether or not it was as precious to me. What would my attitude be if I were in danger of losing my faith? Would that loss hurt me enough to bring tears or would I consider it too unimportant to be concerned? I found no rest until after I had given satisfactory answers to these questions.

PRAYER: Our Father, may our faith be such a priceless possession that we will develop it, never permitting it to wane. May we find courage to hold steady no matter how strong the forces arrayed against us seem to appear. In Jesus' name. Amen.

THOUGHT: A faith that fails us when we need it most could already be lost.

63. WHAT A FRIEND WE HAVE IN JESUS

Ye are my friends, if ye do whatsoever I command you." (JOHN 15:14)

Trouble followed him wherever he went. The first great blow came at home in Ireland, when his intended bride accidentally drowned on the day before their wedding date. He was never in robust health and the shock of this tragedy remained with him the rest of his life. His desire to become a soldier ended when he was physically unable to meet the strict requirements. At the age of 25 he decided to move to Canada and serve Christ in some way there. It was a total commitment of his life in service to the poor and needy and those physically unable to care for themselves in Port Hope, Ontario. He even gave them his own garments when he had no money to give. He ministered to the sick as though they were his own family. Some considered him queer. They were unaware of the influence of Jesus on his life. Those who really knew him erected a monument in his memory after his death. They knew that he had brought more comfort to more people in this poverty stricken area than the majority who walk the highway of contentment and peace.

It was while ministering in Port Hope that he again fell in love and wedding plans were made. Once more tragedy struck when his fiancee died after a brief illness.

He was now 35 years old and he received word that his mother in Ireland was facing a severe crisis. In loneliness and sorrow he unburdened his soul before the Lord. He came to the conclusion that the only real friend that both he and his mother had was Jesus. He must remind her in some way of that. Taking pen and paper, Joseph Scriven (1820-1886) wrote the words to one of the most comforting hymns ever written. He called it "Pray without Ceasing." We know it as "What a Friend We Have in Jesus."

Tragedy followed Scriven to the end. In his last illness, while delirious, he left his sick bed and going outside, fell in a near-by creek and drowned.

What a friend we have in Jesus,
  All our sins and griefs to bear!
What a privilege to carry,
  Everything to God in prayer!
O what peace we often forfeit,
  O what needless pain we bear,
All because we do not carry,
  Everything to God in prayer!

* * * * * * *

Where will we meet this Friend today? Anywhere, because He is everywhere. It could be when we stand before the crib of a new born baby. He will be there, and we will not only open our heart to this precious gift of God, but to Jesus who is there to bless us. We could meet this Friend on a bed of pain. He will be the Comforter standing beside our bed to encourage and to heal us. It could be when sorrow enters our life. He will offer us then the hope of Eternal life. Or it could be in His church. Why do worshippers feel renewed when they worship? Why do others go to the altar for prayer? They have met Jesus, and they go to Him with their problems and spiritual failures. But why wait for any of these experiences? He is where we are on all occasions and there is something wrong if we do not sense His presence daily.

Do you have problems or burdens that are difficult to bear? Go to Jesus; no one can have a better friend. Go to Him in simple faith and say, "Jesus, I need you as my friend." Miracles will then happen and you will become a new person.

PRAYER: Heavenly Father, thank you for sending us the best friend we could ever have. We know that all other worth-while friendships are the result of His influence upon their lives. In the name of this dear Friend we pray. Amen.

THOUGHT: When has Jesus ever ceased to be our friend?

64. SWEET HOUR OF PRAYER

"We will give ourselves continually to prayer, and to the ministry of the word." (ACTS 6:4)

"Sweet Hour of Prayer" was written by a man who knew the meaning of prayer. Being blind, William W. Walford, (1772-1850) received the insight and strength he needed to minister and work in the area in which he felt God had called him. Although he was a shopkeeper, and much of his income was received from this source, he also was ordained and did considerable preaching. He created many useful articles out of bone and ivory in spite of his blindness. Little else is known of this gifted man, but his name will live through this hymn that has touched the hearts of multitudes.

These words might never have gone any further, were it not for the Reverend Thomas Salmon, an English Congregational minister who upon hearing the words asked for a copy. He was on his way to America and after arriving had Walford's poem published in the *New York Observer* in 1845. In this way it came to the attention of

William B. Bradbury, who with his brother later manufactured the Bradbury pianos. He composed music for many hymns and he was soon busy composing music for these words which he completed in 1859. It later appeared in our hymnbooks and for over a hundred years has brought comfort and consolation to multitudes of devout Christians.

Sweet hour of prayer! Sweet hour of prayer!
  That calls me from a world of care,
And bids me at my Father's throne
  Make all my wants and wishes known;
In seasons of distress and grief,
  My soul has often found relief
And oft escaped the tempter's snare
  By thy return, sweet hour of prayer!

* * * * * * *

Early one morning before the turn of the century, a young man hunting on bleak Labrador, left on what almost ended in his last trip. Hauling his boat across the ice to open water, he sighted his quarry, raised his gun and fired. Unexpectedly the boat capsized throwing him in the icy water. At that precise moment, his mother in Newfoundland, awoke with a start. Certain her son was in danger she knelt and prayed earnestly that he would be saved.

As she prayed, another man in that far off ice field was hurrying in the opposite direction. He heard cries from the ocean, but deciding it was birds he continued his journey. After a few more steps, however, something compelled him to turn in the direction of the water. Later he said, "I felt there was some unknown power leading me on." Upon reaching the sea, he saw the drowning man whose cries no longer could be heard, and rescued him.

How could a mother, hundreds of miles away, know that her son was in danger? How could her prayer turn another person against his will to change the direction in which he was going to the place where he could rescue her son? I do not know entirely, but God is doing this repeatedly. This, however, I do know: that mother was my grandmother; the drowning man, my father, and I have preached the gospel for forty-four years because God heard and answered that mother's prayers years before I was born.

Believe me when I say, "I believe in prayer!"

PRAYER: Our Father, we have prayed for many things and when the answer comes we sometimes fail to give you the credit.

Help us to know that you want us to take you at your word. In Jesus' name. Amen.

THOUGHT: Prayer has not changed. God's ability to hear and His desire to answer ever remains the same.

65. PRAYER IS THE SOUL'S SINCERE DESIRE

"O thou that hearest prayer, unto thee shall all flesh come." (PSALM 65:2)

James Montgomery (1771-1854), a layman, was a youth of great talent. Although the son of missionary parents, his idea of life was to enjoy it to the fullest. He made complete use of his opportunity to enter into the social life of his day. He was also very independent and for a time a free-thinker.

His Moravian missionary parents died in the West Indies while ministering to the people there. This had a decided effect on their son. His talent was revealed very early. He began writing poetry at ten and continued in this endeavor until his death. Having left school at fourteen he went to work in a bakeshop. It wasn't long before he tired of this daily routine. At sixteen he left with not much more than the clothes he wore and some poems he had written. He managed to sell one poem for a guinea which enabled him to survive until he found another job.

In 1794 he became owner of "The Sheffield Iris", a newspaper known for its independent views. Montgomery was only twenty-three years old at the time, and still fiercely independent. Six months later he was arrested because of a poem he wrote and had printed in his paper, hailing the fall of the Bastille in Paris. He was given a three month sentence and fined $100. He spent his time amidst the dirt of the Sheffield prison writing poetry. Upon his release he went back to his newspaper as unrepentent as ever. As a result, two years later he was again jailed and this time given a six month sentence and $150 fine. On this occasion he spent his time writing a book entitled, "Prison Amusements."

He was forty-three years old before he accepted Christ and was readmitted into the Moravian Church. From then on instead of devoting his time entirely to his newspaper he championed various much needed reforms such as the outlawing of the slave trade and advancing the cause of foreign missions. He also became the author of some of the best known hymns of the church. Among them a beautiful hymn on prayer. The hymn has been sung to many tunes.

Prayer is the soul's sincere desire,
  Uttered or unexpressed,
The motion of a hidden fire
  That trembles in the breast.

* * * * * * *

What do you expect when you pray? If your prayer is worthy and sincere you should expect an answer. You should expect to receive an inner peace. Storm clouds might be everywhere, but prayer lifts these clouds and you can go on living as though they never existed. You should expect strength when you pray. No matter how weak you are God can and will supply the strength you need. You certainly should expect your burdens to be lifted. You and I are responsible for many of our burdens and prayer helps destroy that which causes them. When you pray expect to be made unselfish and kind and be given love to embrace the unlovely. When you are sick in body stand upon God's word and expect to be healed. Jesus is in the business of bestowing upon you the best things for your life. All you have to do is put your faith to work and ask.

PRAYER: Have Thine own way, Lord! Have Thine own way;
Search me and try me, Master, today!
Whiter than snow, Lord, wash me just now,
As in Thy presence humbly I bow. Amen.

THOUGHT: Prayer is still the prelude to power.

66. DEAR LORD AND FATHER OF MANKIND

"Be still and know that I am God: I will be exalted among the heathen, I will be exalted in the earth." (PSALM 46:10)

The quiet young poet was incensed by man's inhumanity to man. It made no difference who was responsible for the pain inflicted upon another, he had to fight it and condemn it. He couldn't turn his back as others did. As a result he was called the poet of the oppressed, but not everyone accepted his views. He was a simple, pious person, yet in the early 1800's he was enmeshed in controversy. Nevertheless, the young Quaker was elected to his state's legislature. This indicated the respect his fellow-townsmen had for him, for members of his denomination at that time were not held in high regard.

He was well known in Massachusetts, the place of his birth, for in 1831 his "Legends of New England" had been published and widely read. Two years later, however, many were bothered by his essay on slavery with a view to its abolition. It was received with mixed emotions and even some of his close friends wondered if this youthful poet and essayist would ever get anywhere. Danger loomed before him but he courageously backed the position he had taken. He never once considered the possible harm his stand might have on his future as an author.

For the next fifteen years he wrote thirty-eight poems on the subject of freedom. He is best known, however, not for these pieces but for his other works. He turned his attention toward the men who had to work hard for a living and the legends and stories of America. From his pen came poems that caused others to remember the past, such as "Snow Bound." John Greenleaf Whittier (1807-1892) stirred the hearts of America and the world in many directions, including freedom of man and the peace and serenity of a simple life.

Whittier was deeply spiritual and wrote numerous poems based on Biblical themes. Nine of his hymns appear in our denominational hymn book. Perhaps the most popular and beautiful of his hymns contain these words, "Drop thy still dews of quietness, 'till all our strivings cease," written in 1872. One can sense the Quaker background in these and other words of this hymn.

Dear Lord and Father of Mankind
  Forgive our foolish ways;
Reclothe us in our rightful mind,
  In purer lives Thy service find,
In deeper reverence praise.

* * * * * * *

Our youngest daughter had listened attentively to the prevacation sermon on "The Voice of God." Sometime later we were picnicking on Martha's Vineyard's South Beach. Carefully we selected the day that we might watch the aftermath of the storm that had just ended. Dianne was frightened. The noise of the pounding surf was terrifying to her. Suddenly, however, we became aware that her fear had entirely vanished. Nothing was said until we were leaving and her mother asked why she was no longer fearful. In her usual quiet way she replied, "Because I heard God's voice above the storm."

We are living in a day when, for many, world upheavals appear louder than the voice of God. As a result, their lives are controlled by fear rather than faith. Others can distinctly hear God's voice above the noise and confusion created by man. A serene Christian life is always a testimony that the voice of the Eternal is never silenced. God does speak and blessed is that person who, with complete confidence and faith, listens and obeys.

PRAYER: Our Father, we are thankful that your voice cannot be stilled. In that assurance rests the hope of the world. May there be gladness in our hearts and eagerness upon our lips as we once again say, "Speak, Lord, for thy servant heareth." In the Master's name. Amen.

THOUGHT: Because God speaks to me, I must also be a voice for Him.

67. MORE LOVE TO THEE

"When they had dined, Jesus said to Simon Peter, Simon son of Jonas, loveth thou me more than these? He saith unto him, yea, Lord; thou knoweth that I love thee." (JOHN 21:15)

She was never a strong woman, yet was a prolific writer. Her many successful books followed articles and poems sent to the *Youth's Companion,* while in her teens. After spending some years as a school teacher she became a minister's wife. Parsonage life was not new to her for she was raised in a parsonage in Portland, Maine.

She was twenty-seven years old when she married Rev. George L. Prentiss. The years that followed were the happiest of her life, for in addition to the love that prevailed in their home, she was blessed with children whom she adored and lovingly cared for. Then eleven years after their marriage tragedy struck in the form of an epidemic that carried away the two children who were dearest to them.

What does one do when tragedy strikes? To whom will we go for comfort? Elizabeth Prentiss (1818-1878) turned to God and then to her Presbyterian minister husband. During the weeks that followed, with her grief unabated she asked the universal question, "George, why should this happen to us?" He reminded her that the more they loved and trusted God, the quicker their sorrow would end. Later as she sat alone, reading her Bible, these words of her husband took on greater meaning. Love, more love was what was needed, George had said, so in the midst of her tears she reached for her note paper and began to write a poem on love for Christ.

She had nearly completed her poem when she decided it was not worth finishing. It was not equal to her earlier works, she thought, so she put it aside without even mentioning it to anyone. In 1869, thirteen years later, while attempting to dispose of odds and ends of paper that had accumulated, she came upon the poem that had long been forgotten. She read it over and decided to show it to her husband before disposing of it. He insisted upon her finishing what she had begun and after receiving the completed poem, had copies printed. Someone sent a copy to William H. Doane, who composed the music and published it in a song book he had prepared.

More love to Thee, O Christ,
  More love to Thee!
Hear thou the prayer I make
  On bended knee;
This is my earnest plea,
  More love, O Christ, to Thee,
More love to Thee, more love to Thee!

* * * * * * *

I met her early one morning in an elevator on the way to the 10th floor. She was singing, "More love to Thee, O Christ, more love to Thee." She stopped only long enough to say "Good morning," or "Have a good day," as she let her passengers in or out on each floor. As I looked around me, I noticed the majority were men, hats off, quietly listening. In that crowded space were Catholics, Protestants, Jews and perhaps an unbeliever. If she had selected a popular number someone would have kidded her, but there was no levity that morning. She was singing of her love for Jesus, and these men knew they needed that message. They would be under tension all day and these words could be the only calming influence received.

Upon leaving I said, "I am glad to find someone not ashamed to express her faith." She turned a radiant, smiling face toward me as she replied, "No, sir, I'm not ashamed," and I knew she meant it.

It is easy to express one's faith while at worship. However, this day calls for those who are not afraid to take Christ out of the sanctuary and expose Him to a world in dire need of His Gospel.

PRAYER: Our Father, as the storms of life sweep over us may we sense around us the everlasting arms of your love, and the "peace be still" of Your Son. Amen.

THOUGHT: There is nothing Jesus wants more than to be where we are when tragedy strikes.

68. CHILDREN OF THE HEAVENLY KING

"Sing praises to God, sing praises; sing praises unto our King." (PSALM 47:6)

Any young man who followed John Wesley in the hectic days of early Methodism, had to be brave as well as a sincere Christian. It was no job for a weakling or a coward. Yet young men came, were converted and soon were impatient to go out and face the angry mobs that threatened them everywhere. One of these young men was John Cennick (1718-1755).

Like many in that day one would not choose him for religious work. He had a somewhat reckless nature, was carefree and spent much time in reckless pursuits. His idols were cards, the play house and reading trashy novels – all sinful pastimes in his day. Eventually he sickened of these things and began to set his own spiritual house in order.

While walking the streets of London one day, meditating on the change that should take place in his life, he suddenly heard the words, "I am thy salvation." He knew that only the Lord could convey that message and from that moment he began to prepare himself for the ministry. Although the grandson of a Quaker, he was drawn to the evangelism of the Wesleys. At twenty-one he was standing beside other courageous preachers in front of angry mobs preaching the gospel. The routine was usually the same wherever he went, eggs breaking against his body, drenched to the skin by fire hoses, paint splattered over his garments and rocks causing blood to flow from wounds on his face. Yet he pleaded with his listeners, always reminding them of God's love and urging them to flee the wrath to come.

He wrote many hymns during his stay with the Wesleys, among them, "Children of the Heavenly King." He later ministered to the Moravians, still persecuted because mobs didn't like them either.

Children of the heavenly King,
  As we journey let us sing;
Sing our Saviour's worthy praise,
  Glorious in his works and ways.

* * * * * * *

Running through the Bible is a word we often overlook and neglect. That word is praise. Praise is the prelude to spiritual power. Yet so many feel that because they sing hymns of praise on Sunday morning they have received all the power they need. Nothing could be further from the truth. God expects us to continually praise Him. It is not optional, but a Divine requirement.

Do you need healing? Start praising the Lord. Are you worried, filled with fear, depressed? Keep praising God and give Him an opportunity to lift these burdens and notice how quickly it will be revived. If we want to be a whole Christian let us keep the praise of God on our lips continually.

PRAYER: Heavenly Father, you bless us daily. May we never cease to praise your name and express our love for all that you have done for us. In Jesus' name. Amen.

THOUGHT: Whatever blessings are ours we owe to Him.

69. STAND UP FOR JESUS

"Stand therefore, having your loins girt about with truth." (EPHESIANS 6:14)

The following hymn was inspired by the dying words of a twenty-nine year old Episcopal rector. The newspaper of that day called him "The eloquent and popular divine." He was eloquent and thousands of his hearers dedicated their lives to the Lord under his preaching. However, the popularity of young Dudley A. Tyng was sometimes questioned. He was outspoken, especially on the sins of the day and the evils of slavery. He disturbed his wealthy parishioners to such an extent that he was forced to resign his pastorate. To this group he was not popular, but nevertheless he had a large following who believed as he did, and not many weeks later all of Philadelphia, including many former enemies, hailed him as one of the outstanding clergymen of the day.

Tuesday morning, April 20, 1858, Dudley Tyng left his study to watch the operation of a corn-shelling machine in use not far away. The newspaper account follows. "Stepping on the inclined plane, he placed his hand on that portion of the instrument known as the "mule" which spreads out the corn. His dressing gown became entangled in the wheels of the apparatus, which lacerated his arm from elbow to shoulder, severing the main artery." Five days later he died.

Before his death, however, he pleaded with his physician who was not a Christian, to accept Christ as his Saviour. He then urged his wife to persuade their sons to follow him into the ministry; and to his father, an outstanding Episcopal clergyman, he said, "Stand up for Jesus, father; stand up for Jesus, and tell my brethren in the ministry, wherever you meet them, to stand up for Jesus." He then requested the singing of "Rock of Ages," and as the voices began to wane, Dudley A. Tyng fell asleep.

The next Sunday, George Duffield, Jr. (1818-1888) preached a sermon on Ephesians 6:14 which was a memorial to Dudley A. Tyng. At the conclusion of the message he read a poem he had written after the funeral of the heroic minister. Copies of the poem were printed and one appeared in a religious publication. The author thought no more about it until he later discovered it had been set to music.

Stand up, stand up for Jesus,
Ye soldiers of the cross;
Lift high His royal banner,
It must not suffer loss.

* * * * * * *

It takes courage to stand up for Jesus, not only in places of danger, but before an unsympathetic heart. Sir Wilfred Grenfell, the late missionary doctor of Labrador, once said that the thing Christ seemed to be asking him when he came to the moment of decision was, "Have you the courage to follow me?"

We live daily amidst worldly minded people. Even in our business and social life there are moments when we dare not speak the good words for Jesus that come to our lips. We do not want to be laughed at or shunned. May God help us to stand courageously for that which we believe.

PRAYER: Dear Lord, how much of myself have I given You? Have I allowed You first place in my life? Do I dare stand up for You when others condemn You or take Your name in vain? Search me and try me and reveal to me the areas in which I have failed to stand up for You. Amen.

THOUGHT: The world is waiting for those who dare to live like Jesus.

70. WHERE CROSS THE CROWDED WAYS OF LIFE

"The Lord said unto the servant, "Go out into the highways and hedges, and compel them to come in that My house may be filled." (LUKE 14:23)

"I have never written a hymn and feel certain that I lack the ability to write one for our hymn-book," said Frank Mason North (1850-1935). He had just been asked by Professor Caleb T. Winchester to write a missionary hymn for the forthcoming Methodist hymnal of 1905. The professor was aware of North's poetic ability and considered him to be the proper person to write such a hymn. Finally Dr. North promised to give it a try. His interest was in missions, but at that moment the thought uppermost in his mind was for missionary work in the crowded cities. He knew city life well and understood the problems, dangers and fears that prevailed in every large city. He had watched people long enough to sense the disillusionment, the pain, the sorrow and the sin that hardened their lives. These were the people upon his mind when he sat down to write his missionary poem. However, His thoughts went beyond these troubled lives to the One who was walking with them daily. With compassion he wrote what he called, "A Prayer for the City." We know it as "Where Cross the Crowded Ways of Life."

Where cross the crowded ways of life,
Where sound the cries of race and clan,

Above the noise of selfish strife
We hear Thy voice, O Son of man!

* * * * * * *

Even though there are sore spots in every city there is good there also. God is present and Jesus is walking in every area where sin abounds. He walks the streets of our cities just as surely as He walks the aisles of the church. Wherever we go tomorrow Jesus will be there. The great compassion and yearning of Christ is more evident where the soul is in danger than in any other place. Multitudes of pure minded men and women will be walking the same city streets with the vulgar and the virtuous, and Christ will be in their midst. The church is there also, seeking to minister to those who desperately need help. We are never alone in the city and we are never without help. The Lord is there to guide us and to deliver us from danger.

Hear His word as He speaks to our soul. "Yea though I walk through the valley of the shadow of death, I will fear no evil, for thou art with me." "When thou passeth through the waters I will be with thee . . . when thou walkest through the fire thou shalt not be burned for I am the Lord thy God." "The Lord is in this place and I knew it not." "Where sin abounded grace did much more abound." "This is none other than the house of God, this is the gate of heaven." All of these places are in the city; the valley of the shadow of death, the deep waters, the destroying fire, the place of sin, and in these teeming areas can be seen the gate of heaven. Our God is a great God. He never leaves us alone, and no city can hide us from his sight.

PRAYER: Our Father, we need your guidance daily. Whether we walk the streets of a crowded city or dusty country roads, may we feel your presence. As your love floods our soul, that road can become for us the very gate of heaven. Amen.

THOUGHT: If we cannot see God in the city our spiritual eyesight is not fully developed.

71. ONCE TO EVERY MAN AND NATION

"Blessed is the nation whose God is the Lord; and the people whom he hath chosen for his own inheritance." (PSALM 33:12)

The youth was embarrassed. Although his friends were many he didn't want to be seen by anyone. His last year at Harvard didn't end as he had anticipated. Everything was going along well he thought. His grades were good. He had been named poet of his class which in itself was a great honor. The one thing he disliked was getting up early. Chapel services began as soon as it was light enough to see and that could be any time after five o'clock. He had nothing against going to prayers, but a nice warm bed appealed to him more at that hour.

He might have liked his comfortable bed, but authorities didn't. They reprimanded him and for a while he struggled to attend, but soon his weak efforts ceased and his chapel seat remained empty. Eventually the poet of his class was suspended and finished his senior work at Concord, Massachusetts, under the guidance of Rev. Barzillai Frost. He was humiliated. To make matters worse the budding poet was not even allowed to read his poem on class day and it had to be printed. It is said that James Russell Lowell (1819-1891) rode in a canvas covered wagon to Harvard and peeped through a small opening to see the dancing around the tree.

He studied law, but without much interest. He opened an office in Boston but spent much of his time writing poetry and prose essays. He was appointed to a diplomatic mission in England but nothing seemed to take the place of his first love – writing.

Among his works is the following hymn:

Once to every man and nation
  Comes the moment to decide,
In the strife of truth with falsehood,
  For the good or evil side;
Some great cause, God's new messiah,
  Offering each the bloom or blight,
And the choice goes by forever
  'Twixt that darkness and that light.

* * * * * * * *

During the Iroquois Theater fire in Chicago a young college student was horrified to see strong, husky men trample on women and children in order to save themselves. He did not seek a way out for himself. Instead he broke a window and asked men in the building across the narrow alley to get him some boards that would stretch across the space in between. They were hastily gathered and he built a bridge. Then picking up the panic stricken and injured women and children he carried them to safety. He had saved 18 when his bridge caught fire and he was thrown to the pavement below. As this hero lay dying in a Chicago hospital he said to those by his bedside, 'Don't feel sorry for me. Some men don't get their chance to live until they are 60. I have had my chance at life and I am not twenty. Christ wanted me to do it, and I did."

"Once to every man and nation comes the moment to decide." That moment came to young Will McLaughlin in the Iroquois Theater disaster where he had gone to enjoy the Christmas performance of "Bluebird." The moment of a great decision can come any time, anywhere. Will we be ready for it? Will Jesus be so real to us that we will immediately know what he wants us to do? The time to make certain is now, before that hour of decision comes.

PRAYER: Lord, make me alert to your voice that I may clearly hear and obey your word when my moment of decision comes. In your name I pray. Amen.

THOUGHT: God forgive us when we are no longer concerned over the needs of our brother.

72. AMERICA THE BEAUTIFUL

"Righteousness exalteth a nation; but sin is a reproach to any people." (PROVERBS 14:34)

In 1893 Katherine Lee Bates (1859-1929) an English teacher at Wellesley College, was asked to lecture at the Colorado College in Colorado Springs. That summer, with a group of teachers, she stood upon Pike's Peak admiring the beautiful view that surrounded her. As she looked down at the scenery below the words of a song were born. After reaching Colorado Springs she completed her poem and two years later it was published in *The Congregationalist.* Although it was given various tunes it was not until put to the music of "Materna" that it began to catch on.

"Materna" was composed by Samuel Augustus Ward in 1882 for the hymn, "O Mother Dear, Jerusalem." Set to this music the hymn became so popular that a move was made to make it a national anthem.

Katherine Lee Bates is remembered in Falmouth, Massachusetts, the town of her birth. Her birthplace has become an historic site and the street leading in that direction from Route 28 has been named Katherine Lee Bates Road.

O beautiful for spacious skies,
  For amber waves of grain,
For purple mountain majesties
  Above the fruited plain!
America! America!
  God shed His grace on thee,
And crown thy good with brotherhood
  From sea to shining sea!

* * * * * * *

We don't have to stand on Pike's Peak to realize how beautiful America is. We are blessed by its beauty and the freedom that is ours. But in spite of this America would not be the lovely country that it is, were it not for Jesus Christ who has made that freedom possible. May our love for our country never wane, and our love for Jesus continue to increase daily.

PRAYER: Thank you, our Father, for our country and for your Son in whom is found the only lasting freedom. In His name. Amen.

THOUGHT: God is relying on us to make a better America. We can rely on Him to do His part.

73. MY COUNTRY 'TIS OF THEE

"Blessed is the nation whose God is the Lord; and the people whom he has chosen for his own inheritance." (PSALM 33:12)

The divinity student was bored. He had graduated from Harvard in 1829 and now in 1831 was well advanced in his Biblical studies at Andover Theological Seminary, not far from Boston. It was a dreary February afternoon and not knowing how best to occupy his time he picked up some music books in German, given to him recently by Lowell Mason. They were chiefly books for children's schools, but as he idly thumbed through one book, his eyes rested upon a page in which the music looked both interesting and patriotic. He had no thought of writing a patriotic piece or anything else until he was gripped by the music before him. He was so stirred that within an hour he had written five verses. After much thought he decided to leave out his original third verse. That verse ended with these words, "No more our blood be shed by alien hands."

"I did not design it for a national hymn," said the 23-year-old Samuel Smith (1808-1895). I was led by the impulse of the moment to write the hymn now styled 'America'. Neither did I think it would gain such notoriety."

He reviewed the words again, this time with a shrug of indifference, feeling there would be little interest in what he had written. "I dropped the manuscript into my portfolio, and thought no more of it for months." He did place a copy, however, in the music books he returned to Lowell Mason. Mason was not only the organist at Park Street Church in Boston and composer of sacred music, but was director of music education for Boston's public schools.

Samuel Smith might have forgotten his poem but Mason had not. On July 4, 1831, the author was surprised to hear his song sung on the steps of the Park Street Church directed by Lowell Mason. It was not until some time later that Dr. Smith learned that the music he had selected was the tune of "God Save the King."

My country, 'tis of thee
Sweet land of liberty,
  Of thee I sing;
Land where my fathers died,
Land of the pilgrims' pride,
From every mountain side
  Let freedom ring.

* * * * * * *

Macaulay, in one of his essays tells the story of a Hindu who believed that every drop of the river Ganges was sacred. One day a European gave him a microscope and placed a drop of the Ganges water under the lens and asked him to look. He did and was horrified to discover that his sacred water swarmed with pollution. Did he decide never again to bathe in or to drink of that filthy water? Not in the least. Instead he broke the microscope that he might not see the germs that existed there.

Today, instead of killing the germs that are destroying our nation, home and the lives of our children, too many are breaking God's microscope that they may not see the sins that abound. God has a way of revealing these ugly germs to us in order that we might purify the stream. Too many, however, do not want the stream purified. They are more anxious to enjoy their share of the pollution. In that case, it is not God's microscope but they themselves who become the casualty.

PRAYER: Heavenly Father, we pray that you will bless America in spite of her shortcomings and neglect. We ask also that we may become a blessing, not only to our country, but to a world that is yearning for something better. In Jesus' name. Amen.

THOUGHT: May God save America from the forces that would destroy her.

74. WHEN THE ROLL IS CALLED UP YONDER

"In my Father's house are many mansions; if it were not so I would have told you. I go to prepare a place for you." (JOHN 14:2)

She was a ragged, emaciated, sad faced little girl who sat gloomily upon the porch of her house that was badly in need of repairs. Hunger pains were not new to her, for she felt them daily. Whatever was available at home she had, but with a drunken father she never had enough.

As she sat brooding that day her eye caught the sight of a man approaching, whom at first she did not recognize. He was well dressed and looking at him she knew he was not hungry. She was not sure whether to run or to wait. She had run from strangers before and she knew what happened to some who were not fortunate enough to escape. However, this man was smiling and not cursing like others. She became more puzzled when he called her by name and urged her not to be afraid because he was her friend.

Upon reaching her he extended a kindly hand and began to ask questions. He looked from her to the sordid surroundings, then to her much worn and torn dress. He knew he could help her but could never remove all the difficulties from her path. "I am James Black," (1856-1938) he said, "and I am the teacher of a Sunday School class, and I would like to have you come and visit with us." Looking at her dress she hesitated but gave the assurance that if possible she would be there on Sunday. The next day there arrived at her house a complete new outfit, hat, shoes and all.

The next Sunday she was there, a very happy child dressed in her new clothes. For several weeks she came, even entering in the program of the church. Then one Sunday when the roll was called she was absent. James Black was concerned. What if some tragedy had befallen her and she would never again answer the roll. That thought haunted him as he walked home. As he entered the house the words of a hymn came to him and going to the piano he immediately set them to music. It was not until later he learned that this child had been taken sick and a few days later died.

When the trumpet of the Lord shall sound,
  And time shall be no more,
And morning breaks, eternal, bright and fair;
When the saved of earth shall gather over on
  the other shore,
And the roll is called up yonder, I'll be there.

* * * * * * *

The pastor was late entering his pulpit for the Sunday morning service. An alert usher made his way to the study and found the preacher looking across the tracks of his large city, and weeping. He was overwhelmed by the poverty and need that he knew existed there. Seeking to console him the usher said, "It is sad, sir, but in time you will become accustomed to it." The pastor replied, "That is why I am weeping. I will become accustomed to it!"

It is always a tragedy when we become so immune to the anguish of others that we lose our concern for them. James Black couldn't get accustomed to the sordid surroundings and the pathetic plight of a little girl in the back alleys of Williamsport, Pennsylvania. Like Jesus, he had to do something about it.

Everywhere Jesus went he faced the needs of the people and had compassion upon them and ministered to each according to his condition. To the blind he gave sight. To the despondent he gave hope. To the weak he gave strength. To the disturbed he gave peace. To the sorrowful, comfort, the unbelieving, faith, the sinful, forgiveness, and the dying, life everlasting.

PRAYER: Our Father, you have planned well for our lives. The plans of men would leave out so much, but you leave nothing to chance or to men's thoughtlessness. Before the earth was fully formed, you had our future well planned. That is why everything you do is so beautiful. In the name of Jesus we thank you. Amen.

THOUGHT: Death does not take from us anything that is worth keeping.

75. ABIDE WITH ME

"They constrained him, saying, Abide with us; for it is towards evening, and the day is far spent." (LUKE 24:29)

He was never a robust individual. In fact, most of his life the shadow of tuberculosis hovered over him. He was born in a Scottish home of poverty and left an orphan when only a child. As he grew older his great desire was for an education, but receiving what he wanted proved to be a difficult experience. Like so many other determined young men, he finally reached his goal and at the age of twenty-one was ordained and appointed to a small Anglican parish in Ireland. In 1823 he was transferred to the church in Lower Brixham, Devonshire. There he labored until his death.

In spite of his failing health he was a hard working curate and as gentle and pure as a child. The heavy responsibility at Brixham proved too much for his weak constitution. Through the years it was thought he wrote one of the church's most beloved hymns while on his death bed. Recently, however, it was discovered that the words began to form in his mind many years before although he did not commit them to paper until near the end of his life.

In the course of his ministry he was asked by a dying brother minister to come and pray with him. During the time spent together both clergymen received a conversion experience. Just before they parted his sick friend took his hand and with tears in his eyes, pleaded, "Abide with me. Abide with me." As he left the house these words remained with Henry Francis Lyte (1793-1847) and a poem began to form in his mind but he soon put the idea aside to finish later. His busy life prevented him from completing the work at the time, although he managed to write several other hymns, one concerning his own heart warming experience while ministering to his sick friend.

His final years were devoid of happiness and the work proved too much for his weak constitution. Ill health caused him to spend much time away from his parish and some of his parishioners left and joined another church. On his last Sunday he served communion, then retired to a favorite spot on the nearby beach to finish the poem he had delayed writing for so long. The spread of his own disease influenced what he wrote for he realized how much he needed the Master to abide with him. Every verse of this hymn-prayer suggests the approaching end of his life. He returned at sunset and while his family thought he was resting, he was in his study putting the finishing touches on his immortal hymn. The next morning he left with his family for Nice, France, expecting to regain his health. Instead he died in less than two months. He lies buried there in the English Cemetery and on his gravestone are carved these words:

"Heaven's morning breaks, and earth's vain shadows flee,
In life, in death, O Lord, abide with me."

Abide with me; fast falls the eventide;
The darkness deepens; Lord, with me abide!
When other helpers fail and comforts flee,
Help of the helpless, O, abide with me.

* * * * * * *

It is hard to understand how a person can endure suffering apart from Jesus. Many times have I heard some timid soul say, "Pastor, will you pray for me?" I understood, for I knew that no matter how dedicated their doctors and nurses might be they needed something more. They needed Jesus. His touch could not only bring healing to the soul but to the body as well. Henry Francis Lyte needed more than human companionship or even the ministry of a dedicated physician. He needed the touch of the Master upon his life.

Are your burdens this moment more than you can bear? Are you suffering from some illness that seems to go unchecked? If so, remember that Jesus has the answer. He has promised to share your burdens as you go to Him for rest. He does more than that for He heals multitudes daily of the most fearful diseases. All He asks is that you have faith and that you are willing to stand upon His word. Anything is possible to him who believes. If you are not healed physically He will give you the necessary strength to face the future unafraid.

PRAYER: Our Father, when we become discouraged or fearful may we not run here and there for relief. May we first go to you and believe that we have received what we prayed for, and according to your word it will be ours. In Jesus' name. Amen.

THOUGHT: Our greatest victories are often achieved through life's most painful experiences.

76. NEARER, MY GOD, TO THEE

"And he dreamed, and behold a ladder set upon the earth and the top of it reached to heaven. And behold the angels of God ascending and descending on it." (GENESIS 28:12)

Can any good come out of a jail sentence? For the most part the answer would be "No," but there have been exceptions. Perhaps in this case the exception resulted in one of the church's most popular hymns. Oh, the hymn was not written in jail, and the person jailed was never the author, but without what happened during that period of incarceration the way would not have been cleared for the hymn that came 42 years later.

It happened in this fashion. A bishop's political pronouncements were severely criticized by Benjamin Flower, who was the editor of the *Cambridge Intelligenser* in England. As a result of that criticism, Bishop Watson made certain that Flower would spend some time in jail. This happened in 1798 during the French Revolution, and Flower not only condemned the bishop but defended the Revolution. There were many who sympathized with the jailed editor and during his time behind bars he had some visitors, among them Miss Eliza Gould. Her attention to him didn't cease with the first visit, for before long she had fallen in love with him and eventually they were married.

One might wonder at this point what all the above has to do with one of the church's most beloved hymns! Well, as a result of the romance that began in jail, that led to marriage, also led to a daughter born to them seven years later. That daughter they named Sarah, who in turn married a man named Adams. Then in 1840, a Unitarian, Sarah Flower Adams (1805-1848) wrote the hymn, "Nearer My God to Thee," to conclude a sermon her pastor was to preach on Jacob's dream, the following Sunday.

Sarah became a talented actress and a theatre success. She gave up this promising career, however, because her strength was not sufficient for the many hours involved. Later she died of tuberculosis, contracted from her sister whom she faithfully nursed.

Nearer, my God, to thee, nearer to thee!
E'en though it be a cross that raiseth me;
Still all my song shall be, nearer my God to thee,
Nearer my God, to thee, nearer to thee!

* * * * * * *

God will supply our needs, not only physically and materially, but spiritually. How many of those around us owe their salvation to our influence in leading them to Jesus? How many have felt power oozing from our lives? If we live near enough to God that is what will happen. If we have yielded our lives to the Eternal, we have been given God-like power. The problem is we are not using what has been freely given us. In fact, many of us have never suspected that power is there. Let us claim these soul-saving gifts that are rightfully ours, and go forth and be a blessing.

PRAYER: O, Lord, help us this day to so live that no act of ours shall cause us to depart from your presence. We want to draw nearer to you and avoid anything that will separate us from your love. In Jesus' name. Amen.

THOUGHT: The closer we draw to the Lord, the nearer we come to our fellowmen.

77. SUNSET AND EVENING STAR

"I am the resurrection, and the life; he that believeth in me, though he were dead, yet shall he live." (John 11:25)

His years were nearly spent, yet Alfred Lord Tennyson (1809-1892) wanted to take another sea voyage. He was a deeply spiritual man and the Bible was his daily companion. Every time he took communion he felt the presence of Jesus, and he never lost the consciousness of that presence. Once while walking on the beach he said to his niece who was walking with him, "God is with us now . . . just as truly as Jesus was with his two disciples on the way to Emmaus."

His last sea voyage was an enjoyable occasion and during which he found time to write the poem, "Crossing the Bar." His son later said that the moaning of the bar was on his mind as he continued to write. After dinner he showed the finished poem to his son for his examination. After carefully reading it he passed it back to his father saying, "That is the crown of your life's works." Tennyson said that the thought came to him in a moment and the Pilot was "that Divine and unseen who is always guiding us."

Three years later the poet was dead, but just previous to that hour he asked his son to put "Crossing the Bar" at the end of all editions of his poems. "The life after death is the cardinal point of Christianity," he said. Shortly after, he asked the doctor if death was near, and when the doctor nodded, Tennyson said, "That's well." Crossing the bar held no dread for him.

Sunset and evening star,
And one clear call for me,
And may there be no moaning of the bar
When I put out to sea.

* * * * * * *

Upon the death of her mother a friend said to the family doctor, "I wish I could go to sleep and not wake up for a year." His answer was, "It would do you no good, for when you did awake you would still have to go through what you now face." When loved ones leave us, this desire is universal. However, we who have passed through this bitter experience know that we must outlive sorrow. We cannot outsleep it.

Grief leaves a wound upon our heart in much the same way as an injury leaves one upon our body. As the wound on our body heals, so does the wound in our heart. The scar remains, but scars are only an indication that there was once pain. God can heal even the sorest wound. He, however, does more. He develops as He heals. It is often in sorrow that God makes a life whole.

PRAYER: Our Father, in the midst of sorrow may we be aware of the hand that brings healing to our broken heart. This we ask through Jesus Christ our Lord. Amen.

THOUGHT: God never takes from us what He has given in love. He but keeps them for us, a reminder that they are ours always.

78. NOW THANK WE ALL OUR GOD

"Enter into his gates with thanksgiving and into his courts with praise; be thankful unto him, and bless his name." (PSALM 100:4)

It would seem that the hymn, "Now Thank We All our God," was written in a surrounding of peace and serenity. Such was not the case. It was written by Rev. Martin Rinkart (1586-1649) who spent horrifying days with very little rest burying over four thousand victims of the plague, including his wife. It happened while he was arch-deacon in the town of Eilenberg during the Thirty Years' War. With the war came the plague of 1637, and Eilenberg, being a walled town became a haven for refugees fleeing from both the war and disease. This contributed to the over-crowding that in turn led to famine and greater sickness.

To add to the woes of those still alive, several invading armies of the Thirty Years' War, marched through their town inflicting cruelty and demanding tribute money. This happened not only once but on three occasions, each time sacking more of the town and demanding more money from the inhabitants, most of whom were reduced to poverty. Punishment was also meted out to the citizens because of the cool reception given the invaders. Rinkart's own material losses were so great that he was barely able to secure enough bread and clothes for his children. Yet in the midst of this condition he wrote this happy hymn of Thanksgiving.

Now thank we all our God
  With heart and hands and voices,
Who wondrous things hath done,
  In whom his world rejoices;
Who from our mother's arms,
  Hath blessed us on our way
With countless gifts of love,
  And still is ours today.

* * * * * * *

My most impressive Thanksgiving lesson was received from one who was blind from birth. It didn't happen on Thanksgiving, but at Easter. I was the assistant pastor of a church in Watertown, Massachusetts, and taught a large Sunday School class. That class was composed of teenage boys with several from Perkins Institute for the Blind. The lesson dealt with Nature's resurrection in the spring to be followed by the resurrection of Jesus. However, before I finished the first section, a blind boy interrupted, saying that during the week a group from the school had gone on a hike through the woods with one of their teachers. His enthusiasm grew as he said, "The trees and flowers were so beautiful I didn't want to leave." It was with difficulty that I finished the lesson, for my home was on the edge of the same woods and I walked these paths every day. I had seen each tree and flower he so vividly described, yet only gave a hurried glance as I passed by.

Although possessing the necessary sight to witness the never ending miracles of God each day, I realized that I did not possess the same thankful heart or rejoicing spirit of that youth. My prayer that morning was that God would open my eyes that I might see, and my heart that I might rejoice.

PRAYER: Thank you Father, for the spirit of Thanksgiving you have placed in the heart of each of your children. May we ever keep that rejoicing heart. In Jesus' name. Amen.

THOUGHT: Jesus found something for which to be thankful even in the face of seeming defeat.

79. ANOTHER YEAR IS DAWNING

"He that sat upon the throne said, Behold I make all things new." (Rev. 21:5)

She was a soul winner. At forty-two years of age she died, but during those years she did more to lead people to Christ than most who live twice that long. When fifteen she committed her life to the Saviour and of that experience she said, "Earth and heaven seemed brighter." It was not only earth and heaven that took on a new luster. From that moment on this became the story of her life.

Some time later she enrolled in a school in Dusseldorf where she finished at the head of her class. Finding no one with whom she could meet with for Bible study or prayer, she declared, "I do not think there is one beside myself who cares for religion."

She had a real gift for languages and had no trouble talking to the people she met in her travels. She could carry on a conversation in six languages and authored many volumes of fine work. In the small towns and villages she did what she liked most, preaching, distributing Bibles and visiting the sick and shut-ins.

In 1874 Frances Ridley Havergal (1836-1879) published her New Year's hymn, "Another Year is Dawning" on a greeting card intended for her friends. However, it went beyond that and eventually found a place in the hymnals of most denominations. Five years later she died but her hymns will live as long as people worship.

Although she possessed a weak constitution and was ill the latter years of her life, her hymns and poetic work indicate activity, especially activity for the Lord. Wherever she went she earnestly spoke to others about their soul. "Another year of service, of witness for Thy love," was not just a poetic expression. She practiced it. As one of her publishers said, she had a "deep and earnest faith, a loving self-surrender to the Saviour."

This New Year's hymn has been sung to several tunes.

Another year is dawning,
  Dear Master, let it be,
In working or in waiting
  Another year with Thee.

* * * * * * *

I watched a group of children at play. They apparently had been playing for some time and their feelings were ruffled. In childish fashion each was accusing the other of cheating. Finally one assuming the role of peacemaker, quieted the others saying, "Let's begin again and this time let's play fair." These words could well be our motto for the New Year.

Let's play fair, especially with God. He is still touching the lives of men daily. He is in every amazing thing we take for granted. These miracles occur daily but we so often do not recognize the source from which they come. He has made possible man's flight into space and the knowledge that seeks to prolong life through heart transplants. No matter how thoughtless we have been He has an answer for our problems. That answer will always be based on love.

PRAYER: Our Father, You are the one who makes all things new. May that newness come to Your world, Your church and our lives this year. In Jesus' name. Amen.

THOUGHT: Let's begin again, and this year let's play fair with God.

80. OTHERS

"The things that thou hast heard of me among many witnesses, the same commit thou to faithful men, who shall be able to teach others also." (2 TIMOTHY 2:2)

General William Booth was appalled by the misery of the poor. His one desire was to help them, to find employment for the unemployed, to rehabilitate the alcoholics and clean up the dens of prostitution. This desire came early in his life. At thirteen he was apprenticed to a pawnbroker, and he watched those who brought in their possessions. He was aware that they were often parting with cherished articles.

At seventeen he became a lay preacher, but not wanting to continue preaching on a circuit, he later withdrew from that branch of Methodism. It was at that point he entered a ministry that was dear to his heart – serving the poor in the large cities. No denomination at the time did much to help the destitute. He sought help from the church but met abuse instead.

He began a movement he called, "Christian Mission to the Heathen of our Country." That ministry opened in a tent in the east end of London. Eventually it became the Salvation Army. He was persecuted, ridiculed and condemned for his unorthodox methods. However, the work grew. He and his courageous wife, Catherine, could not be stopped no matter how great became the opposition.

One Christmas General Booth wanted to send greetings to all the Salvation Army officers throughout the world. He never had extra money to work with at any time but on this occasion it was almost nonexistent. He knew he couldn't afford the greetings he intended to send, so he began cutting his message down. Finally one word kept repeating itself in his mind. That word was "others" and discarding everything else he had written, it was this one word alone that was sent throughout the world.

Later C. D. Meigs was so impressed by this one word Christmas greeting that he wrote a touching hymn-poem that was set to music by Elizabeth McE. Shields. The chorus follows:

> Others, Lord, yes others,
> Let this my motto be,
> Help me to live for others,
> That I may live for Thee.

* * * * * * *

How many dark spots dot our pathway of service! There was the person whom we knew to be desperately sick. We were aware of the unfinished work in that home, the tired ones who ministered, the desire for companionship and words of comfort, but we were too busy.

How many are better this moment because of us? Because we have loved them enough to minister to their needs? How much concern do we have for the suffering of others, especially those who seem unattractive to us? It is a sad day when a follower of the Master never hears the sobs of mankind. When he becomes so blind that he cannot see the tears of suffering. Or when he is so full that he cannot understand the pain of an empty stomach. William Booth selected a very important word for his message. How important are we making that word?

PRAYER: Dear Lord, help us to live for others, that we may live for Thee. Amen.

THOUGHT: Multitudes are waiting to see Christ. Are we helping to show Him to them?

81. GOD OF THE STRONG, GOD OF THE WEAK

"When thou hast eaten and art full, then thou shalt bless the Lord thy God for the good land which he hath given thee." (DEUT. 8:10)

He was no longer young but his heart still yearned for those less fortunate than himself. What was it like to be blind? His friend, Helen Keller, was blind. How did such a long night of darkness feel? He wanted to find out, so he was blindfolded and led to a wintergreen berry patch located on a rough and rocky hillside. In complete darkness he groped for the illusive berries. It was not easy. His hands were scratched in his search as he stumbled around in his pursuit. Finally he touched what he was seeking and scooping up the berries, he removed his blindfold saying, "If I had to do anything skillful it would have gone hard with me."

What was it like to live in a dismal and dangerous tenement? He called these buildings of New York "slaughter houses," especially the rear tenements that became a death trap to those who lived in them. More than half of the fires of the city were in these crowded houses. He was not satisfied to read about these disasters, he had to see them for himself. After a long day's work therefore, he would go out at night in fireman's rubber coat, helmet and badge, in all kinds of weather until he secured the information he sought, then he would launch a vigorous movement of reform.

He forever worked to change bad situations. He was one of the most courageous men of his day. Yet Richard Watson Gilder (1844-1909) was a quiet man who wrote poetry and challenging editorials. One woman said that he could say "no" more graciously than some men could say "yes."

He was also a man of God. Andrew Carnegie called him the sweetest, saintliest and one of the most heroic souls he had ever met. "God, Christ, immortality, sin and sorrow were constantly in his brooding," said another. This is reflected in the hymns he wrote. I quote from one.

> God of the strong, God of the weak,
>   Lord of all lands and our own land,
> Light of all souls, from Thee we seek
>   Light from Thy light, strength from Thy hand.

* * * * * * *

I remember reading some years ago the words of a reporter who was covering a banquet attended by many of the nation's outstanding leaders. He stressed the noise and confusion caused by the rattling of dishes and the loud conversation that prevailed. Then the master of ceremonies pounded on the rostrum for quiet. The noise gradually ceased. Waiters were in their places waiting for the signal to rush forth with food for the table. When it became quiet enough a clergyman took his place and offered an appropriate prayer. The moment the "Amen" was said the din began all over again, as every one turned to the business of eating. The reporter ended his account with these disturbing words. "Now that God was out of the way these leaders could get down to the business of the evening."

These words are terribly distressing because this is too often what happens. After the prayer is over – after God is out of the way, men proceed as they always have. The result is that the world is continually in a state of confusion.

However, God hasn't changed. As He spoke to men in Biblical times so also does He speak to us in this day. He is still the God of the strong and the God of the weak. He cannot be pushed out of the way or ignored. He is speaking through all of today's turmoil and also directly to our soul if we would listen.

PRAYER: We are often frightened, our Father, by the screaming headlines of our day. We often fail to hear your still, small voice.

Teach us that real power does not come from the loud, destructive voices of the world, but from your voice of gentle stillness. In Jesus' name. Amen.

THOUGHT: Our faith may falter but not God's faithfulness.

82. BRIGHTEN THE CORNER

"Thus sayeth the Lord: Refrain thy voice from weeping, and thine eyes from tears, for thy work shall be rewarded, saith the Lord." (JEREMIAH 31:16)

Our dreams do not always become a reality, but we can turn our disappointments into songs of faith. Ina Dudley Ogdon's dream was to use her voice for the glory of God. She wanted a singing career, but she also wanted to be an evangelist. However, she never made either.

At the very beginning of Ogdon's debut the message came that her father was ill and to please come home. From that time on she ministered to an invalid father and was busily engaged in the household duties. Her home was not a very bright spot, but she was determined to make it so. She wrote hymns, both for her own enjoyment and for that of others. Perhaps the most familiar is that which grew out of her own experience, "Brighten the Corner Where You Are." Homer Rodeheaver selected this hymn as the theme song in the Billy Sunday meetings. Ina Ogdon's name as a singer or evangelist would not be known today; instead, she lives through the hymn that has brightened unknown thousands of corners the world over. The music was written by Charles H. Gabriel, whom Methodist Bishop Joseph H. Berry called in 1926 the foremost composer of Christian songs of this generation.

"Do not wait until some deed of greatness you may do,
Do not wait to shed your light afar.
To the many duties ever near you now be true,
Brighten the corner where you are."

* * * * * * *

How often we failed to brighten someone's life because we waited too long. We meant to seek forgiveness from the one we injured, but we put it off. We intended to write a letter to a friend we knew to be despondent, but we had so much else to do that the letter was never written. We planned to call on the sick, but our day's activities left no room. Our intentions were good as we faced numberless opportunities to be of service. Then the day came when our all-but-forgotten plans could no longer be fulfilled. We were too late, and our belated words sounded hollow and our offers of assistance soulless. Let us stop procrastinating and start brightening corners where we live.

I thought of how heedless and selfish
We are to our friends, small and great,
To walk past their doors when they need us,
Then send them our flowers—too late! G.W.W.

PRAYER: May we be sensitive to the needs of others, our Father, that we may be your hand extended to them while their need is greatest. In Jesus' name. Amen.

THOUGHT: The best rest for the weary comes in ministering to others who are weary.

83. WHEN HE COMETH

"And they shall be mine, saith the Lord of Hosts, in that day when I make up my jewels; and I will spare them, as a man spareth his own son that serveth him." (MALACHI 3:17)

One of the most drastic things that can happen to a preacher is for him to lose his voice. This happened to Rev. William Orcutt Cushing (1823-1902) who quite early in life felt the Lord had called him into the ministry. Without hesitation he went through the necessary course of study and was ordained. Then he lost the use of his voice and he became aware that the pulpit ministry was out, but what would he do? Praying earnestly that God would still use him in some form of Christian work, he waited for the answer. It wasn't long before he received the gift of hymn writing. He never realized before that he possessed this ability, but as he began to write poems seemed to flow from his pen. In time his completed hymns began to appear in current hymn books. As a preacher he would probably be an unknown today but as a hymn writer his name still lives upon the pages of many hymn books. Of the many he wrote I have picked one for children called "Jewels," written in 1856. I remember singing it lustily in Sunday School when it was quite popular. It still has a warm place in my heart.

When He cometh, when He cometh To make up His jewels:
All His jewels, precious jewels, His loved and His own.
Like the stars of the morning His bright crown adorning,
They shall shine in their beauty, Bright gems for His crown.

* * * * * * *

Little lives are molded daily
By the rules you keep or break;
Little feet move ever closer
To the maze of steps you take.
What you are they never question
Whether you be false or true,
And that boy or girl who watches
Plans some day to be like you.

Little hands are ever reaching
For the things your hands first hold;
Little heads are always storing
What their ears and eyes behold.
Will your actions safely keep them
Pure in thought and word each day?
Or your careless conduct send them
On a sordid Christless way?

Little lives are fondly dreaming
Of the years that stretch ahead,
When they take their place beside you
And they walk where you have led.
What you do will be their practice;
What you say will be their speech;
Have you built a strong foundation?
God-like goals for them to reach?

–G. W. W.

PRAYER: Our Father, as parents You have given us a great and awesome ministry. We are responsible for the spiritual and physical development of each child. May our own desires never interfere with our responsibility to them. In the Master's Name. Amen.

THOUGHT: Blessed is the home where right living predominates, genuine love demonstrated and Christian character molded.

84. RESCUE THE PERISHING

"For the Son of man is come to seek and to save that which was lost." (LUKE 19:10)

William H. Doane, composer, had some thoughts concerning the words he needed for a hymn tune he had just finished. For some time he had been brooding on the subject of "rescue the perishing." Many composers could also write their own verses, but Doane was no poet. He therefore had to get someone else to write the words. There was only one logical person to his mind, Fanny J. Crosby (1820-1915), and as on other occasions he found that she was the right choice. She was not only the author of many hymns as early as 1869, but was also interested in the souls of wayward men and women. Her blindness did not keep her away from Rescue Missions of New York. It was not unusual to hear her ringing testimony as she stood before the ragged and often odorous congregation. She also spoke on street corners and open air meetings.

She said, "I was addressing a large company of working men one hot summer evening, when the thought kept forcing itself on my mind that some mother's boy must be rescued that night or not at all. So I made a pressing plea that if there were a boy present who had wandered from his mother's home and teaching, he would come to me at the close of the service." The service ended and a young man eighteen years of age came forward and asked, "Do you mean me? I promised my mother I would meet her in heaven, but as I am now living that will be impossible." Fanny, in her loving way talked kindly to him and then prayed. After they arose from their knees there was a new light in the youth's eyes as he said, "Now I can meet my mother in heaven, for I have found God."

That boy was on her mind as she returned home and remembering the request of William Doane to write a hymn on "Rescue the Perishing," she not only started the poem that night but had finished it before retiring. The next day she had sent it to Doane, who, she said, "wrote the beautiful and touching music to my hymn as it now stands."

Rescue the perishing,
Care for the dying,
Snatch them in pity from sin and the grave;
Weep o'er the erring one,
Lift up the fallen,
Tell them of Jesus the mighty to save.

* * * * * * *

Howard Thurston was one of the world's great magicians. When he was a boy his father severely whipped him. In anger he ran from home and disappeared. It was five years before his family heard from him. During that period he was arrested dozens of times, shot at and driven from one town to another. At seventeen he was a derelict of the streets, penniless and stranded in New York. He drifted into a religious meeting in time to hear the preacher say, "There is a man in you." For the first time in his life he was stirred, and two weeks later, this former boy hobo was on the street corner of Chinatown preaching.

There is a man in us and his name is Jesus. No matter how great our sin might be he will forgive us and start us on the right road again. When Jesus is accepted and lives in us, we can weather the greatest storms, whether we foolishly brought them upon ourselves or they suddenly appeared in the road before us.

PRAYER: O God, people are perishing all around us. They are not just in the area of Rescue Missions, but are often our next door neighbors. You must wonder if we care enough about their plight to be willing to cross the street or go next door to minister to them. Instill in us the desire your Son placed in the heart of His disciples to seek and save the lost. In Jesus' name. Amen.

THOUGHT: When one who has slipped has been revived, or a soul drawn near the kingdom, it matters not to Jesus whether it has been done through the efforts of a minister or a consecrated layman.

85. ETERNAL FATHER, STRONG TO SAVE

"The disciples came to him and awoke him, saying, Lord, save us; we perish." (MATTHEW 8:25)

Years before our navy used the hymn, "Eternal Father, Strong to Save," it was being sung on English ships. William Whiting (1825-1878), the author, was born in London and during his career became Master of Winchester College Choristers' School. He was not only thinking of the dangers of the sea, but was addressing his stanzas to the Father, Son and Holy Spirit. The last words of the first three verses, not only have a universal appeal to sailors, but for those waiting for their return home, "O hear us when we cry to Thee for those in peril on the sea."

Not much more is known of William Whiting. He seemed to have spent most of his life on shore, and his profession would not include a ministry to seamen. Yet he was well aware of storms, shipwrecks and loss of life, for Winchester was only 72 miles from busy Southampton port. He was greatly concerned for those who sailed in dangerous waters, where tragedies occurred almost daily. During his lifetime ships in trouble had no means of calling for help and sometimes it was weeks or even months before the loss of a vessel was known.

Eternal Father, strong to save,
Whose arm hath bound the restless wave,
Who bidst the mighty ocean deep
Its own appointed limits keep;
O hear us when we cry to thee,
For those in peril on the sea.

* * * * * * *

In the same year, 1860, that the above hymn was being written in England, a sea tragedy was occurring on Lake Michigan. The steamer, *Lady Elgin,* was rammed by the schooner *Augusta* in a sudden thunderstorm, and was rapidly sinking. The captain headed toward shore, hoping he could beach the side-wheeler, but the damage was so great that reaching land was impossible. She was so near and yet so far for any would-be rescuers to be of any help.

However, in the group of on-lookers was a young divinity student, Edward Spencer, from Northwestern University. He was a good swimmer and fifteen times he plunged into the rough waters, saving fifteen men and women from drowning. He was about to go out to the wreck again when he collapsed from exhaustion. With his remaining strength he managed to drag himself to a spot where he could build a fire and get warmed. This respite didn't last long for as he looked out over the water he saw a man attempting to reach shore while trying to hold on to another person. Instead of remaining by the fire, he plunged into the cold water again. The couple he saved were a husband and wife. Unable to make another trip he kept repeating over and over, "Did I do my best? Did I do my best?"

Over 300 lives were lost that day, but there would have been 17 more if Edward Spencer had not done his best. This is what the Lord expects of us. We might not be able to save those in peril on the ocean, but there are millions in peril on the sea of life, and as Christians we are called upon to do our best to save them.

PRAYER: Our Father, lead us in the pathway of service that we may be more alert to the needs of others. We know that we are not called to be life-savers of those in danger on the sea, but we are expected to reach out a hand to those sinking under the sea of adversity, sickness, sorrow and sin. Dear Lord, help us to do our best. Amen.

THOUGHT: He who stilled the raging waters of Galilee has never lost His power.

86. JESUS, SAVIOUR, PILOT ME

"He maketh the storm a calm, so that the waters thereof are still." (PSALMS 107:29)

In the days when ships had no means of communication other than distress signals, shipwrecks were a common occurrence. As late as the winter of 1909-1910, the *Boston Post,* under the headlines, "Furious Winter's Wrecks," contained a long list of vessels that after leaving their home port were never heard from again. The list of dead was staggering and was but a continuation of what went on in the centuries before. In a three-month period during that stormy winter the *Post* listed fourteen schooners lost with all hands aboard. As a result of these many disasters hymns concerning the perils of the sea were written and sung by multitudes who understood. One, "Jesus, Saviour, Pilot Me," is still a popular hymn today.

This hymn was written by a man who understood the dangers of the sea. Rev. Edward Hopper (1816-1888) was a Presbyterian clergyman who ministered to sailors. He also wrote poetry. In the early 1870's he finished a poem about the sea and the danger of tempestuous storms that blow over the lives of every individual. Later he sent it to the *Sailor's Magazine* but decided not to sign his name.

On May 10, 1880, the anniversary of the Seaman's Friend Society was to be held in New York City. Rev. Hopper was asked to prepare a hymn for the occasion. He remembered the anonymous poem he sent nine years before to the *Sailor's Magazine* and presented that as the hymn-poem to be used. For the first time the author of a much used and loved poem was known. It was accepted and given a previously composed tune by John Edgar Gould.

Jesus, Saviour, pilot me
Over life's tempestuous sea;
Unknown waves before me roll,
Hiding rock and treacherous shoal;
Chart and compass came from Thee:
Jesus, Saviour, pilot me.

* * * * * * *

Richard Halstead was a flippant young sailor who went with his shipmates to the Seaman's Bethel, Vineyard Haven, Massachusetts, because he had nothing else to do. When Chaplain Madison Edwards, my wife's grandfather, questioned him, Richard decided he would shock him. He recited his moral lapses, his hard drinking, his love of gambling and the role of women in his life. Madison heard him through and soon Richard found he was before a man who could shock also. The Chaplain told the story of the prodigal son and then reminded Richard that he was on the same road.

After leaving the Bethel Halstead told a companion, "I don't want my life to be like that." A sleepless night followed and an equally trying day. The next night he was back at the Bethel, only the third time he had ever been to a religious meeting. When the Chaplain asked who would yield their lives to Christ, Richard's hand was raised higher than any other.

Three quarters of a year passed and Madison received a letter from Richard saying he was coming home in order to prepare himself for helping others as the chaplain was doing. He did come home but not as expected. Off Nantucket the boat he was on sank and during the ten hours he was adrift in the life-boat he froze to death. With tears he could no longer suppress, Madison wrote, "This dear boy is lying in death in the Bethel tonight." The next day he tenderly prepared him for burial, and later laid him beside a saintly old seaman who had been buried in the Bethel cemetery not long before. Richard's homecoming was not as a prodigal but as a young seaman saved by the grace of God.

PRAYER: Our Father, not only do we ask for insight to see ourselves as we really are, but also a desire to seek Divine forgiveness. Teach us that only as we place ourselves in your hands will we be lifted above self. May we not continue to follow the imperfections of man, but rather the flawless life of your Son. Amen.

THOUGHT: No matter what we have done, God always has a word for us. We can rest assured that word is based on love.

87. THROW OUT THE LIFE-LINE

"The men rowed hard to bring it to land; but they could not: for the sea wrought, and was tempestuous against them." (JONAH 1:13)

In the early years of the Life-Saving Service the crews trained faithfully every day. Monday was cleaning-up day at the station, a day for keeping in order whatever equipment needed repairs. Boat drill usually came on Tuesday; on Wednesday, practice in code signals. The next day would see training with the beach apparatus: how to use the breeches buoy and to load, sight and fire the Lyle gun that shot the life-line to a wrecked vessel.

The Rev. E. S. Ufford (1851-1910), a New England Baptist minister and evangelist, watched such a drill by the crew of the Life-Saving Station at Point Allerton, Nantasket Beach, Mass., in the fall of 1886. He was intrigued by the firing of the life-line, especially when one of the crew demonstrated how it was used. On arriving home after this experience, Ufford wrote the words of "Throw Out the Life-Line" in fifteen minutes, and composed the melody shortly thereafter. It was later published in sheet form but was not widely used until Ira D. Sankey purchased it and turned it over to George C. Stebbins to rearrange and harmonize the tune.

Throw out the life-line across the dark wave,
There is a brother whom some one should save;
Somebody's brother! Oh, who, then will dare
To throw out the life line, his peril to share?

* * * * * *

Although the life-line saved many sailors' lives, the life-saving crew was not always successful. It was not because they didn't try, or gave up because of a failure. As members of the Life-Saving Service they were commissioned to save lives; so are we as Christians called upon to save souls. Our job is to rescue the perishing who are foundering in the sea of life. The world is full of young and old who, after making a mistake, have allowed it to grow until they become overwhelmed by the storms they have created. Every such individual could be saved if we were as anxious to throw out the life-line of the Gospel as the life-saving surfman is to reach those wrecked at sea. As Christians we are a rescue team and the Word of God is our life-saving equipment.

PRAYER: Lord, may we yield our lives to you, for we never know when the seas of life will overwhelm us. Amen.

THOUGHT: God has given us His Word as a life-line to aid those who are floundering in life's seas.

88. LET THE LOWER LIGHTS BE BURNING

"Let your light so shine before men, that they may see your good works and glorify your Father which is in heaven." (MATTHEW 5:16)

The preacher, with great earnestness, was describing a devastating storm on Lake Erie. As his audience eagerly listened, he told of a conversation between a concerned Captain and his pilot.

Because only the light from the lighthouse could be seen in the distance, he asked, "Are you sure this is Cleveland?"

"I am very sure," replied the pilot.

"I cannot see the lower lights," said the captain.

"They have gone out, sir," was the reply.

More concerned than ever the captain asked, "Can you make the harbor?"

"We must or perish, sir!"

The pilot took a stronger grip on the wheel and looked steadily ahead but it was too late. Because the lower lights were out he missed the channel and the boat smashed against the rocks and many lives were lost.

"Brethren," continued Dwight L. Moody, "the Master will take care of the great Lighthouse. It is our job to keep the lower lights burning."

Philip P. Bliss (1838-1876) was so deeply stirred by the famous evangelist's illustration that before he went to bed that night he wrote both words and music to this popular gospel song.

Let the lower lights be burning!
Send a gleam across the waves;
Some poor fainting, struggling seaman
You may rescue, you may save.

* * * * * * *

For over fifty years my father-in-law, Austin Tower, was chaplain of the Seaman's Bethel in Vineyard Haven, Massachusetts. Working with him was his faithful wife, Helen, who was not only a missionary to the seamen, but a mother to the thousands of sailors who visited the Bethel yearly. The hymn the sailors most often called for was, "Let the Lower Lights be Burning." Chaplain Tower would tell them that the ministry of the Bethel was to keep the lower lights burning for them and all seamen. He reminded them that somewhere that very night many would be in dangerous waters. Every listener understood because they had been through the same experience. They could relate to that. Many were the times when on a stormy or foggy night, all eyes were strained landwards, eager to catch the glimmer of lights along the shore.

But the chaplain told of another meaning of this hymn, a meaning which came alive as they sang the verses. God our Father constantly beams His love and mercy upon us, but He gives to us the responsibility of keeping this love-light burning in our lives for the benefit of those about us who may be tempest-tossed or lost in darkness. "Thousands have sat here as you do tonight, and are now scattered all over the world. Some are in dangerous waters. Others, whose anchor grips the solid rock that is Jesus Christ, are safe."

The greatest thrill that came to these devoted missionaries was leading hundreds of young seamen to Christ each year. At the end of his message the chaplain would ask "Are there any who would like to take Christ as their pilot?" On one occasion a *Vineyard Gazette* reporter was present and later wrote, "It was a sight to make a Christian heart rejoice to see the uplifted hands." These dedicated missionaries kept the lower lights burning!

PRAYER: Oh Lord, we might not be seamen, but we know what happens when lights go out. May we never cease in our labors of keeping the Gospel lights burning all over the world. In Jesus' name. Amen.

THOUGHT: Christ has ignited a flame in us. May we never allow it to be extinguished.

89. THE NINETY AND NINE

"If a man have a hundred sheep, and one of them be gone astray, does he not leave the ninety and nine and goeth into the mountains, and seeketh that which is gone astray?" (MATTHEW 18:12)

Some hymn writers never lived to see their hymns in print. Elizabeth Clephane (1830-1869) who wrote the "Ninety and Nine," was one of these. As her regular contribution to "The Children's Hour" she had written a poem on the parable of the lost sheep.

Ira D. Sankey, a composer of sacred music, while in Edinburgh with Dwight L. Moody for evangelistic meetings, saw the poem reprinted in a religious periodical and cut it out for possible future use. Not long after, during one of the meetings, Moody, who was about to preach on the Good Shepherd, called his organist-soloist aside and whispered, "sing something." Sankey thought of the poem in his vest pocket, but he hadn't as yet set it to music.

Music, however, was no great problem with this outstanding musician, so he placed the poem on the organ and began to play and sing. His eyes had to be glued on the unfamiliar words while at the same time he composed a tune. The melody came and continued throughout this hymn, in the presence of over a thousand people, who had no idea a new hymn was being composed as they listened.

When Sankey ended, tear dimmed eyes were seen throughout the audience, but Elizabeth Cecilia Clephane who had written the poem was not there to hear it. She had died of tuberculosis five years before.

Sankey was so overwhelmed with the reception the hymn had received that he was on the verge of tears. Speaking of this experience later he said, "It was the most intense moment of my life."

There were ninety and nine that safely lay
  In the shelter of the fold,
But one was out on the hills away,
  Far off from the gates of gold –
Away on the mountains wild and bare
  Away from the tender shepherd's care,
Away from the tender shepherd's care.

* * * * * * *

An English preacher tells of a new church that was built during his pastorate in London. When they came to the pulpit steps they found that it was necessary to make the first step higher than usual. It was a source of danger, for strangers often stumbled, not realizing it was higher than the other steps. Therefore, whenever the minister invited a guest to preach or take part in the service, he would always say to him, "Beware of that first step." This is the advice people have been getting from God since the very beginning, yet so many have failed to listen. One step leads to another until they become lost sheep.

What are we as Christians doing about this important problem? What are we doing about the stray sheep that might be living in our neighborhood? Whatever our thoughts are about this ever increasing number, may we not allow our prejudice or indifference to encourage them to nibble their way to destruction. Let us tell them the story of Jesus. He is their only hope.

PRAYER: Our Father, we need to be protected from ourselves. It is not the evils of the world that destroy us, but our own sins. Help us to be honest and place the blame where it belongs. In Jesus' name. Amen.

THOUGHT: We never can be happy by doing what we know to be wrong.

90. GOD BE WITH YOU 'TILL WE MEET AGAIN

"The Lord watch between me and thee, when we are absent one from another." (GEN. 31:49)

"God Be with You Till We Meet Again" is a parting hymn that has blessed multitudes. For years it was thought that Rev. Jeremiah E. Rankin (1828-1904), a Congregational minister born in Thornton, N. H., wrote these words for use as a benediction for the newly-formed Christian Endeavor Society. It was, no doubt, used by this Society shortly after the hymn was published, but the fact is that Rankin wrote it for his own use. By 1880 his Sunday evening service had become an important part of the church program, and he wanted to end the service with a good farewell hymn. None in use satisfied him, so he decided to write his own. Remembering that "good-bye" really meant "God be with you," he went to work on the poem. Rankin had no idea that what he wrote would ever be used beyond his own church, and even after William Gould Tomer added his catchy tune, Rankin never realized it would soon be sung throughout the world. Yet this benediction hymn was almost immediately described as a "farewell with a spiritual thrill in it."

God be with you till we meet again!
By His counsels guide, uphold you,
With His sheep securely fold you;
God be with you till we meet again.

* * * * * * *

My first wife passed away while still very young. The first meeting that I attended after her funeral was a woman's organization, at the time called the Ladies Aid. I sat quietly trying to concentrate on what was going on, but my mind was not on that meeting. My wife was not in her usual place taking an active part as she always did. The women, knowing how I felt and meaning well, began to sing, "God Be with You Till We Meet Again," for my benefit. It was not easy for me and struggling to keep back tears I tried to sing with them. At the moment I wished they had selected another hymn, but on further reflection I knew they were right. That is exactly what Elsie would have said to me if she had the opportunity. She would have smiled and said, "Darling, God be with you till we meet again".

It is never easy when loved ones leave us. Neither is it easy to leave familiar places and friends behind when duty calls us elsewhere. Let us remember that we go not alone. Our greatest Friend will be with us. He will also be with those whom we leave behind and will guide and strengthen them until we meet again.

PRAYER: Thank you for your presence, our Father, wherever we go. With You and Your Son in our life all will be well, for Jesus promised never to leave or forsake us. In His precious name. Amen.

THOUGHT: Jesus will sustain us in our hour of need and support us when we stumble.

ABOUT THE AUTHOR

George William Wiseman graduated from Boston University with the degrees of Bachelor of Religious Education, Bachelor of Sacred Theology and Master of Sacred Theology. For forty-four years he served churches in the New England Southern Conference, the New Hampshire Conference, and the Florida Conference of the United Methodist Church. He is married to Miriam Tower, daughter of the late Chaplain Austin Tower of the Seaman's Bethel, Vineyard Haven, Massachusetts.

They have three daughters, Joanne, teaching in Iola, Kansas; Donna Chapman, residing in Davisburg, Michigan; and Dianne Danielson, of Lake City, Florida.

He is the author of three books, *Life Begins with Faith, Life Begins with Jesus,* and *They Kept the Lower Lights Burning*. He has also written for numerous religious periodicals and his works appear in *Who's Who in Poetry in America, Masterpieces of Religious Verse, Worship Resources for the Christian Year, Prayer Poems,* and many other books.

With his wife he now resides in Lake City, Florida.

www.ingramcontent.com/pod-product-compliance
Lightning Source LLC
Chambersburg PA
CBHW021153020426
42331CB00003B/41
9781621710325